PORT PHILLIP BAY

WILLIAMSTOWN

MELBOURNE ROAD

GEELONG

WESTGATE FREEWAY

Westgate Freeway

WHITEHALL ST

GEELONG ROAD

FOOTSCRAY

ROAD

NORTH OURNE

Melbourne

Melbourne

SOPHIE CUNNINGHAM

NEWSOUTH

A New South book

Published by
University of New South Wales Press Ltd
University of New South Wales
Sydney NSW 2052
AUSTRALIA
www.unswpress.com.au

National Library of Australia
Cataloguing-in-Publication entry
  Author: Cunningham, Sophie, 1963–
  Title: Melbourne/by Sophie Cunningham.
  ISBN: 978 174223 138 9 (hbk.)
  Subjects: City and town life – Victoria – Melbourne.
            Wildfires – Social aspects – Victoria – Melbourne.
            Melbourne (Vic.) – Social conditions.
  Dewey Number: 994.51

Design Josephine Pajor-Markus
Cover Sandy Cull, gogoGingko
Cover photo Ben Ong
Author photo Virginia Murdoch
Endpaper map David Atkinson, handmademaps.com
Printer Everbest

This book is printed on paper using fibre supplied from plantation
or sustainably managed forests.

Contents

Foreword

My mother remembers that when she was a little girl, just after the Second World War, she would go to her grandmother Lucy Wawn's house in a suburb of Melbourne that Lucy called Windsor but was really Prahran. Lunch was announced with a gong. Twenty-five years and a suburb away, I lay in bed at my grandmother's house in the darkness before dawn, listening to the heavy clop-clop of the Clydesdale's hooves as milk was delivered in glass bottles from a horse-drawn cart. My grandmother lived in an avenue that had been built over a spring, and water used to bubble up through the asphalt on a regular basis. This – the Clydesdales, the bubbling spring – was not so long ago: 1971, when I was eight years old and Melbourne's population had just reached 2.5 million.

It's impossible to isolate which of my memories are generic and which are the ones that only a life lived in Melbourne could yield. Or when our memories stop being simply personal and start sounding like echoes of something more: floods remind us of repressed rivers, creeks and billabongs; a falling bridge suggests a parochial city's struggle to become something else; wearing an orange T-shirt emblazoned with 'It's Time' suggests a political watershed, optimism; a footy match is easily understood as class warfare.

I watched Neil Armstrong take his first steps on the moon when I was in prep at Toorak Central School, and a photo of me transfixed by the event was published in the *Sun News-Pictorial*. Summer holidays seemed to be the time that the most inexplicable things happened. On 12 January 1976, Eloise Worledge, a girl not much younger than me, was snatched from her Beaumaris bedroom in the night, never to be seen again. Almost exactly a year later, two young women, Suzanne Armstrong and Susan Bartlett, were found dead at their home in Easey Street, Collingwood. They had been stabbed dozens of times, and the cries of Suzanne's baby son had alerted neighbours to the deaths some three days later. These crimes forever coloured my feelings about both the bayside suburb of Beaumaris and the unfortunately named Easey Street.

For many years, when I was in my early twenties,

friends and I shared a house a few doors up from the one in which Helen Garner set her semi-autobiographical 1977 novel, *Monkey Grip*: 'In the old brown house on the corner, a mile from the middle of the city, we ate bacon for breakfast every morning of our lives'. Well, rumour has it that it was a few doors up. Almost everyone I know claims to have lived near that house, and I've never been able to work out if we're all talking about the same one. The place I'm thinking of is on the corner of Falconer and Woodhead streets in Fitzroy North. As Garner had done some years earlier, I used to ride through the Edinburgh Gardens to the hundred-year-old Fitzroy Pool, a place where the water is not just deep but, as the sign says, *profonda*. I lived in that house with Sarah Mathers, whom I think of as a particularly Melbourne woman. She does magical things with gardens and with food, and as a long-term housemate I was the beneficiary of those skills.

Around 9.30 pm on 9 August 1987, Sarah and I were both at home, only a few blocks from Hoddle Street, when I heard helicopters overhead and turned on the television news to hear that a man had positioned himself, sniper-style, on a raised platform behind the billboard on the corner of Ramsden and Hoddle streets and was picking people off with a rifle. Nineteen-year-old ex-Army boy Julian Knight was finally arrested about forty-five minutes later in McKean Street, around the corner from us. Seven people died that night; nineteen others were seriously injured. It is impossible for me to drive down Hoddle Street without recalling the massacre – an unfortunate way for Melbourne's first surveyor-general, Robert Hoddle, to be remembered.

The cityscape has become embroidered over the years with impressions of these larger public dramas, moments that nestle alongside more private and fleeting experiences. Songs are written, films are made. The layers build until to write about the place where you grew up feels practically like an archaeological dig. Melbourne is a city that, for me, provokes emotions as complicated as any 45-year-old marriage.

With the exception of seven years spent in Sydney, I've lived in Melbourne my entire life. It feels like a small town to me, though in reality it no longer is. I was born at the Royal Women's Hospital in

Carlton, which is approximately 300 metres from where I worked until recently and a couple of kilometres from where I live in Fitzroy, Melbourne's oldest suburb. I began my professional life in Cecil Street, Fitzroy, at publishing house McPhee Gribble. Hilary McPhee, my former mentor and now friend, lives only a few doors from me. A couple of blocks away is Betty Burstall, now in her eighties, who founded Carlton's La Mama Theatre in the 1960s and is the widow of film director Tim Burstall. John Timlin, former literary agent and a long-time administrator of another Melbourne theatrical institution, the Australian Performing Group at the Pram Factory, is down the road. Around the corner, the literary critic Peter Craven works late – he's visible from the street, his desk piled high with books and cats. Our shared friend, the film critic Philippa Hawker, lives less than a kilometre away in Carlton. My girlfriend Virginia and I live in a house once owned by James Button and his wife May Lam, and James is significant to me because he introduced me to my team, the Geelong Football Club. Lead pencil marks charting how quickly the Button-Lam children grew still adorn our living room wall. Like many of my friends, James used to work at *The Age*, the oldest remaining Melbourne daily, founded by David and Ebenezer Syme, the grandfather and great-uncle of my great-grandmother Lucy Wawn (she of the dinner gong). When I first met James, almost twenty years ago, he lived about six houses away from this current house, which is next door to a place I shared for a few years with W.H. Chong, the designer of the covers of my two published novels and also a former designer of *Meanjin*, the literary journal I went on to edit between 2008 and 2010.

At times, it's all felt too close. Attempts to escape the straitjacket of eastern and inner Melbourne include choosing Monash University rather than the University of Melbourne, fairly constant travel and a move interstate. Thus there is a certain irony in the fact that in recent years I found myself in a job that is about as Melbourne as you can get. *Meanjin* was founded in Brisbane by Clem Christesen in 1940 but moved to Melbourne towards the end of the Second World War – both to enjoy the patronage of the University of Melbourne and because Melbourne seemed a better fit given Christesen and the journal's interest in nationalism, culture and poetry. So if my ashes were scattered in the Carlton Gardens you could mount an argument for a life lived as narrowly as that of any 18th-

century English village girl. About 2 square kilometres would cover it. The only strange thing is
that this isn't, really, such an unusual Melbourne
story.

Melbourne's a city you get to know from the
inside out – you have to walk it to love it. My
favourite time to do this is at night. That's when
you capture glimpses of people – eating, laughing,
talking, arguing, watching TV and reading –
through half-open terrace house doors and windows. That's when you see a shaft of moonlight
shoot bright down a bluestone lane, though, as
often as not, by the time you look up to see the
source of the light a cloud has moved across the
sky and the moon has disappeared. It is a city of
inside places and conversation. Of intimacy. It's a
city that lives in its head. It's a city that has winters
grey enough to make most of its inhabitants SAD
and, increasingly, summers punctuated by terrible
heatwaves.

While neither people nor cities can escape their
past, this book attempts to capture the palimpsest
of history, culture, memory, intention and cir-
cumstance that makes up Melbourne today. It is
not a memoir and it is not an autobiography, but
my experiences of Melbourne give it shape. I've

attempted to 'write', if you like, a photograph of the city, or, more accurately, a series of them. And, in as much as I have succeeded in this, these photographs were taken throughout 2009. Inevitably, though, I have touched on events that have taken place since then.

Summer

On 24 January 2009, a group of friends and I visited the Rochford winery in the Yarra Valley (an hour or so out of Melbourne) to hear the legendary Canadian musician Leonard Cohen sing. Australian singer-songwriter Paul Kelly was Cohen's main support act. That day in the Yarra Valley seems more golden in retrospect: twelve days later, fires destroyed more than 4500 square kilometres in north-eastern Victoria. The next concert Rochford hosted was a bushfire benefit – but that was six weeks away.

As I stood with Virginia and looked around the crowd, I saw the faces of many people I'd met in my 45 years: former housemates, current friends, my publisher, ex-lovers, friends of friends, authors I'd worked with, a guy who'd designed the cover of a book I'd once published, the woman who ran my favourite deli stall at Queen Victoria Market, my osteopath. These people create my version of

Melbourne: those looped connections that start in kindergarten, school and university and are refined by where you live and the work you do. In Melbourne the environment contributes to this. Built on a plain, endlessly flat, the city has an appeal that is subtle, while the climate — usually too hot or too cold — is not. (Well, except in autumn. In autumn Melbourne is perfect.) We're turned indoors, towards people. Writer George Johnston said of the place that 'A powerful tide of human dilemma runs beneath the skin of everything'. There's truth to this.

During 2009 I was reading a draft of Paul Kelly's then unpublished memoir, *How to Make Gravy*. A passage from it particularly struck me:

> More and more, my friends and loved ones seem like heroes to me. With them I've shared victories and defeats. Some have risen, some have moved on, some have broken down. We've lost a lot of things along the way. But through it all we've helped each other out — dealing with the illness and death of parents and friends, raising children, looking for love, trying to find good work.

Maybe it is as simple, as complicated, as that: relationships are what make a city.

A week or so before that concert, I'd driven to Yea to do a reading at their library. It's not a long drive, just under two hours if you head north-east of Melbourne, even if you take the pretty, longer route through Eltham, Christmas Hills and Kinglake as I did. Suburbs and country blur in the hinterland — something Melbourne's controversial *2030* planning policy was attempting to manage, with its focus on avoiding inappropriate rural residential development. Eltham is definitely a suburb, but at some indefinable point on the windy Eltham-Yarra Glen Road you slip down into Yarra Glen and you're officially in the Yarra Valley. The road that hugs the eastern side of Kinglake National Park is lined with prehistoric-looking tree ferns and soaring messmate stringybark. Their beauty means you barely resent the large trucks you're inevitably stuck behind on the hilly, single-lane road. Driving slowly allows you to enjoy the view.

I arrived in Yea early enough to have a counter tea with my mum, stepfather and some other locals. We sat around drinking cold beer and talking about the heat. The reading was lively and well attended, and the librarian, Jan Smith, welcomed us warmly. The evening had a personal feeling you don't often find in the city.

A few weeks later, on Saturday 7 February, the temperature rose to 47 degrees Celsius in our street. I tried to fry an egg in the sun but I mistakenly used an aluminium pizza tray, so my attempt to dramatise our plight in an amusing and symbolic way resulted in nothing more than a faint bubble of egg white and a slow hardening of yolk. I uploaded the photos of my failure to photo-sharing website Flickr in an attempt to stay jaunty. But as the temperature rose, so did feelings of anxiety and panic.

That day, which came to be known as Black Saturday, capped off two weeks of above 30- and often above 40-degree temperatures. In the hot weeks of build-up, railway lines buckled, overloaded buses broke down and the then Minister for Transport, Lynne Kosky, looked defensive as she talked of the passing decades and lack of appropriate maintenance under previous governments. It would seem, when all the statistics were done and dusted, that some 374 people died during the heatwave in the last week of January 2009 alone. That's more than twice the number who died in the fires that were to come.

The Cape Lilac tree in our courtyard had a lush green coverage of leaves – it had been planted especially to shade the house in summer and then, when the leaves dropped, let the light in during winter. Usually it made a difference to the temperature in the house, but some leafy shade wasn't going to cut it that Saturday. Over in the Carlton Gardens, possums fell, dead, out of trees. Virginia and I listened as the possum that lived in our roof shuffled about restlessly, trying to relieve its distress. Birds dropped out of the sky.

Birds had also fallen on the wing during the heatwave of 1939. The fires that erupted then resulted in the loss of 2 million hectares of land and seventy-one lives. Despite what had been a century of living through hot summers, people back then sweltered through the heatwave in heavy suits and drank whiskey in dark, overheated pubs. These days we wear light cotton and drink cold beer, but it isn't much compensation for the original layout of the city or the failure of its old-style buildings to effectively fend off rising temperatures.

While the heatwave of January and early February 2009 was the hottest in Melbourne's recorded history, the conditions weren't totally dissimilar to those experienced by early European explorers. When Lieutenant Colonel David Collins arrived at what he called Sullivan Bay (near what's now Sorrento) in 1803, the temperatures were in the mid-forties and he and his party could not find water. Indeed water – the search for it, the corralling of it, the excess of it, the squandering of it, now the lack of it – is a defining motif in Melbourne's history. As was a refusal to build a city that in any way responded to the climate. According to architect and author of *The Australian Ugliness* Robin Boyd, builders and developers in Victoria were

> oblivious to all lessons on the Australian climate
> learnt by the older men in New South Wales.
> In Port Phillip Bay the new settlers found a
> climate milder than any yet encountered on the
> new continent. The winter was grey, damp and
> depressing, but not uncomfortably cold for long
> periods; never cold enough to take leaves for more
> than three months from the English trees which
> they hastily planted ... Despite the lesson of
> the Old Colonials, verandas were not considered
> necessary.

The terrace houses favoured by the boom-era population of the mid-to-late 19th century – a style of house we live in – keep heat at bay for several days, then effectively turn into ovens.

So, we sat in our oven and tried to keep tabs on friends. Cathy, a new friend who'd recently moved to Melbourne from Sydney, went out early to get supplies and then shut herself in her flat with the blind down and wondered to what hell she'd moved. Mike and Ciannon, who live in North Fitzroy, painstakingly covered all the windows of their apartment with cardboard and foil. Susannah and Tom escaped to Aireys Inlet, down the Great Ocean Road, where it was some 15 degrees cooler. Over in Braybrook, Jeff was putting his chickens in the shower cubicle and watering them on a regular basis. I didn't speak to Sian, who lives in St Kilda, but a couple of nights earlier we'd joined her at Elwood Beach, where the temperature at 8 pm was a mere 28 degrees — only to watch, with heavy hearts, the temperature gauge rise 10 degrees as we drove home around midnight. The worms in our worm farm turned into a mass of goo. Our friend Lizzie found her ballroom dancing shoes melted in the back of her car.

Bird, our small Burmese cat who'd been vomiting in the heat, disappeared around midday. Going outside to look for her was like walking into a furnace. Fitzroy is full of old stone terrace houses and high brick walls. In the centre of it, where we live, there are barely any gardens, and only our Cape Lilac and the old gum tree in the yard of the gallery across the road provide any shade or greenery. After two weeks of heat the walls were almost too hot to touch, and the thought of Bird's little pads on the asphalt made me frantic. I scoured the suburb, looking for shady spots she might have hidden in. I even looked in the cellar of the Standard Hotel, the pub a few doors up from us, which she could slip into from the street if she wanted. The barman heard me calling her and directed me out to a tree in the beer garden where she'd dug herself a nest of dirt and was looking quite cool.

The day staggered on. There were phone calls among friends to calm each other; there was chatter online. People photographed the temperature registered on the iconic Nylex clock that sits above the Cremorne silos on Punt Road – 45! 46! – and posted them to social networking sites as proof of suffering.

Virginia and I tried to steel ourselves for the outdoor wedding we were attending at the Melbourne Zoo later that afternoon – about an hour and a half before a cool change was expected. The Melbourne Zoo is Australia's oldest. It opened in 1862, displaying animals that had previously been on public view first at the Royal Botanic Gardens and then at 'Richmond Paddocks' along the Yarra River opposite the gardens. Apparently they'd moved the animals to the current location of Royal Park because they were getting too damp. They wouldn't have minded being damp on that Saturday. None of us would've.

Getting to the wedding was an endurance test in itself. By the time we arrived, my heart was racing, my face was bright red and I was drenched in sweat. I had trouble breathing. We walked from the car park to the large Moreton Bay fig where the ceremony was to take place and I almost fainted. I wasn't the only one. The half-hour or so until the ceremony is a bit of a blur but finally the bride, Keren – who had clearly been kept in a fridge for the day – stepped under the tree, looking cool and elegant. You could see her beautiful pale skin register the shock of the heat as she slowly changed colour over the next few minutes. A temperature drop of 15 degrees around 5 pm saved her. In a Brontë-esque flourish, the bride's and groom's vows had to be shouted above the wild winds that accompanied the change. This was the gale-force south-westerly that caused the long eastern flanks of the fires that had sprung up during the day to join into massive fire fronts.

After the ceremony and before the reception,

Virginia and I took advantage of the more comfortable temperature and went for a walk. The zoo animals were still in recovery, as were we all. The lions were lying on their backs, paws in the air, sprinklers cooling them. The boys' manes ran all the way down their backs and in a tufted line up the middle of their bellies. They looked as shell-shocked as the humans. We walked past meerkats lying flat as pancakes – not a perky sentinel among them.

It wasn't until we got home at midnight that we heard that firestorms had devastated Kinglake, Narbethong, Flowerdale, Marysville and many other Victorian towns. All told, more than 2000 homes were destroyed and 173 people died. No one living in Melbourne was unaffected. For days afterwards people walked around on the verge of tears, stunned. The fires would blaze for several more weeks, keeping a pall of smoke over the city.

Author Peter Temple was finishing his novel *Truth* (which went on to win the 2010 Miles Franklin Literary Award) at the time, and the violent drama of Black Saturday floats through the book like smoke:

> The fire would come as it came to Marysville and
> Kinglake on that February hell day, come with the

terrible thunder of a million hooves, come rolling,
flowing, as high as a twenty-storey building,
throwing red-hot spears and fireballs hundreds
of metres ahead, sucking air from trees, houses,
people, animals, sucking air out of everything
in the landscape, creating its own howling wind,
getting hotter and hotter, a huge blacksmith's
reducing fire that melted humans and animals,
detonated buildings, turned soft metals to silver
flowing liquids and buckled steel.

My stepfather was a teacher at Yea High School.
Many of the students from the school had lived in
Kinglake, where the fires were at their worst. Some
had died. He'd had to — everyone had had to — read
in the paper the details of these teenagers' final
minutes. Jan Smith, Yea's librarian, turned up on
television. She was helping support the displaced
people in the tent city that had sprung up in the
centre of town.

Almost everyone knew someone who'd lost
land, or life, or were worried for areas that had
held the fires at bay and might still go up. Densely
treed rural suburbs, like Eltham, only 20 kilometres from the centre of the city, were on high alert
for weeks, which caused those residents great stress.
People repeated their own, and others', stories over

and over. One of these struck me as particularly apocalyptic: a young man sitting in his backyard in Lilydale watched the fires engulf the area while surrounded by possums, snakes and other wildlife – all seeking refuge.

The media's intense telling and retelling of people's experiences of survival, or of their deaths, became difficult to bear. It was only when researching this book that I realised this relentless going-over of details is a relatively recent thing. Only two days after one of Melbourne's most significant tragedies, the West Gate Bridge disaster of 1970, the horror of what happened when an entire span of the unfinished bridge collapsed had been delegated to page 15. This wasn't because people didn't care: they did, they do, it's an event that haunts the city still. It's just that the culture in which an endless poring over of people's grief, an almost ghoulish fascination with how they 'felt', was not yet the norm in the mainstream media.

It was not long before the distress felt by some victims of the fire shifted to blame – much of it directed at local council policies that had attempted to restrict the amount of clearing allowed on individual blocks of land. There were questions, also, as to whether enough controlled burning had been undertaken in an attempt to cut down on tree litter that acts as fuel for fire. This argument has been had in Melbourne (indeed Australia) since the days of first white settlement. Melbourne is a city that spreads ever outwards. It bleeds into rural areas, following the upper reaches of the Yarra River, the broad arc of Port Phillip Bay. The question of whether we should insist on our 'right' to live in these hybrid habitats has never been adequately resolved.

David Nichols was a neighbour of mine when I was a kid and is now a lecturer in Urban Planning at the University of Melbourne. Twelve days after Black Saturday, he wrote in *The Age*:

> Perhaps we should consider the example of the Gippsland town of Noojee, by all accounts a delightful village in the early 20th century; all but two houses were destroyed there in a ferocious bushfire in the summer of 1926. Within six months, the determined people of Noojee had returned and, with the assistance of well-wishers and supporters, reconstructed a large part of the built fabric of their community. New shops were built and the post office and the railway station were replaced. Trees that were thought to have been killed in the fires grew new leaves, the

wattle bloomed again and the birds returned to the Latrobe Valley. Optimism thrived among the town's inhabitants, as they sought to gain funds for new roads to open up the area for agriculture. This delightful outlook was shattered 13 years later in the devastating 1939 bushfires that wiped Noojee out a second time.

They went on to build yet again.

A few days after Black Saturday, drama of a different kind began to impact upon Melburnians in a symbolic but real way. As a result of the global financial crisis Nylex went into receivership and the lights on the Punt Road clock went out. You may know the clock from Paul Kelly's song 'Leaps and Bounds': 'I'm high on the hill, / looking over the bridge / to the MCG / And way up on high / the clock on the silo / says eleven degrees'. Some twenty years after that was written, shifts in Melbourne's weather had already meant that the clock on the silo was rarely reading 11 degrees and long-sleeved footy jumpers were looking increasingly old fashioned. For the lights to go off altogether seemed more ominous still.

Recently, Fitzroy-based musician and Aboriginal elder Kutcha Edwards, who was stolen from his homelands in Balranald, New South Wales, said: 'When you take from Mother Earth, Mother Earth will seek revenge'. His words were not directed at Melbourne but seem painfully relevant nonetheless. Only four years after John Pascoe Fawkner and John Batman pitched tents by the Yarra River, Melbourne was a town of 10 000 people and a staggering 1.3 million sheep. It was a settlement committed to erasing the landscape that cradled it in the hopes of making something new. This is true of, possibly defines, all cities, but the speed of that destruction in Melbourne was particularly rapid. The first thing the settlers did in 1835, after building their roughly hewn homes, was to dam the Yarra at the waterfall that once fell around where Queen Street in the city now meets the river. Then they cut the wattles that lined the river's shores. Once cattle and sheep were introduced, the Foothill Yam-daisy – a staple food for the local Indigenous tribes – could no longer grow. Those tribes included the Taung Wurrung (north-east over the Great Divide), Watha Wurrung (who lived to the west), Ngurai-IllumWurrung (north-west), Woi Wurrung (usually called Wurundjeri – they lived

23

around the Yarra and its tributaries) and Boon Wurrung (the bay). Collectively, the groups comprise what we now call the Kulin nation – Kulin being the word, in all their languages, for 'human being'.

The clearing of Yam-daisy had catastrophic implications for the Kulin. They were already struggling with a population that had been dramatically reduced by white man's diseases such as small pox, diseases that had moved down from New South Wales before there was even a settlement in Melbourne. (A population estimated to have been as high as 20 000 was reduced to 5000 by the 1830s.) As one Indigenous man described the situation, 'No yam at Port Phillip, too much by one white man bullock and sheep, all gone murnong'. Victorian tribes were also saying that the white man had taken away their rain – that is, the destruction of large stands of trees had resulted in the reduction of rainfall. By 1903, there were only a handful of the Kulin, surviving in the Coranderrk reserve near Healesville, north-east of Melbourne.

However, the burgeoning town of Melbourne was the site of the only attempt in Australia – no matter how misguided and cynical that attempt was – to set out a treaty with the local Indigenous people. And whatever his motivations in initiating the treaty in 1835, John Batman was acknowledging that the Kulin had rights to the land, even if they were rights he wanted to take away. The paths the tribes of the Kulin nation made shape the city still, and the bike trails that now proliferate trace the tracks they used. And latent under the Jolimont rail yards are the remains of the broad wetlands that sustained the Wurundjeri clans. These wetlands sit in the heart of Melbourne and I like to think that heart still beats, albeit weakly, creating a gentle pulse.

Autumn

Come March, Melbourne's dams were polluted by the fires, and water storage was sitting at 30 per cent. The city had been on stage 3a restrictions for two years, which meant cars could only be bucket washed; gardens could only be watered by hand, twice a week, early in the morning; and only a few key sports ovals could be watered. Dedicated gardeners rose at 6 am to water their gardens, or they installed tanks and grey water systems or, like me, saved water from the shower in an odd assortment of buckets that they then used to water their vegies – leading to a syndrome that the Australian Physiotherapy Association dubbed 'bucket back'. People – and public gardens – pulled out their fruit trees, their flowering annuals, and began to return to the native Australian gardens that had been popular in the 1970s. Where European plants were once in vogue, South African plants took over. Succulent gardens were taking off.

Fitzroy residents like to think of themselves as mindful of such things. Indeed, the Greens candidate in the electorate of Melbourne, Adam Bandt, took 45.3 per cent of the two-candidate preferred vote in the 2007 federal election (and went on to win the seat in August 2010). There was schadenfreude in some circles when it was revealed in 2006 that Fitzroy residents were among the highest users of water in Melbourne. This does raise the question of whether a city wanting to reconfigure along more environmentally friendly lines needs to build up its inner suburbs or allow its larger outer suburbs to become more autonomous. Certainly the suburbs are – or can become – greener, and the microclimate that builds up around our treeless centre is not a good thing. David Nichols again:

> The inner-city areas of Australian cities are the conspicuous consumption centres of our society ... while denser nineteenth-century areas of our cities might arguably contain greater potential for environmentally sustainable living, this is really only taking place piecemeal, predicated on individual conscience and motivation. Additionally, food has to be trucked in to the inner areas and sewerage and other waste

transported away and treated; the hinterland is marshalled into service of the metropolis...

Fitzroy was Melbourne's first suburb. It's hard to imagine it now as it was then, when the solitude was described as 'most profound, and though Melbourne is only a short mile distant, so little is its noise carried that way that you might easily fancy yourself far away in the depths of the inland forest'. The area was subdivided in the late 1830s. The houses from those early years have not survived because they were built in a manner befitting an outer suburb – as Fitzroy was for a few brief years – on large blocks, with large gardens. In the 1850s and 1860s rows of terraces went up and Fitzroy now has the largest intact areas of housing from this era left in the city. It also had an enormous number of pubs. It was in Fitzroy's Belvedere Hotel in 1856 that a meeting of stonemasons first called for an eight-hour working day – this was eight years after the publication of *The Communist Manifesto*. The campaign was celebrated on 12 May 1856 with an 8 Hours Procession from the Carlton Gardens to Cremorne Gardens in Richmond, an event that was held annually for the next ninety-five years.

The number of pubs in Fitzroy was not

unusual for the mid-1800s, when hotels were the only places one could buy a meal. What's surprising is that so many of them are still operating – I can count six within a couple of minutes' walk from my house. The historic pubs are surrounded by a large number of bars that have sprung up in the last fifteen years as a result of liquor licensing laws that have, until recently, been kinder in Melbourne than in Sydney.

Fitzroy Street, where I live, is a narrow one-way street that runs from Victoria Parade to Alexandra Parade, parallel to Brunswick Street. It is one of the oldest streets outside the centre of Melbourne. It also had – at its southern end and a century ago – one of the worst reputations. If you stand in the middle of the street and look to the south, you see the city. To the north lie Brunswick and Coburg. Clouds are often banked up high, giving the view in that direction an aura of the tropics. In times of bushfire, a smoky haze usually settles in.

Most people living around us only have small courtyards, if that. So, in warmer weather people in our street often sit outside their houses and share a beer. The boys next door ride their bikes and skateboards up and down, show Virginia their Lego, discuss *Doctor Who* with me and play with young Delphi who lives on the other side of us. This street life, especially kids playing, is one of the things I love about living here, but it was part of the reason the suburb was considered such a disaster by social reformers such as F. Oswald Barnett. His photographs of slums in Fitzroy, Carlton and Collingwood in the 1930s have become iconic images of early Melbourne: a hundred years ago you only lived your life in public if you couldn't afford the space to be private. Occasionally the street is graced by the presence of a tawny frogmouth that makes an appearance outside the pub, perching next to the dangling pair of sneakers. The prevalence of similar dangling pairs all over Fitzroy may evidence the suburb's history as a drug trouble spot – or it could just be a lark.

From the forties, the Fitzroy Council was, reputedly anyway, stacked by John Wren's men. Wren was a boxing promoter, the one-time owner of illegal betting shops and the powerful supporter of Melbourne's inner-suburban and Catholic Labor politicians. (He was also the basis of the character John West in Frank Hardy's 1950 novel *Power Without Glory*.) Wren's grip was firm and held for much of the 20th century. It wasn't until the early seventies that the council included a number of progressive independents from the Fitzroy Residents' Association. They helped save the suburb from a planned freeway that was designed to cut diagonally through Fitzroy from the corner of Nicholson and Johnston streets to the intersection of Alexandra Parade and Smith Street. If that freeway had gone ahead, it would have taken out our street among dozens of others. The FRA was also responsible for many of the roundabouts and one-way streets that now thwart drivers, returning it to the kind of suburb it was almost two centuries ago – a place you walk.

There are certainly always people walking up and down our street, usually towards the Standard Hotel. We hear them comment as they pass our house, usually chatting to and praising our cats. Fitzroy and nearby Carlton are cat suburbs: if you walk the bluestone lanes at night, dozens of glowing eyes look down at you from fences, roofs and trees. It's as if there is a second city, populated by cats and possums, floating just out of our reach. One of the local cats used to live in our house but was abandoned fifteen years ago when the owners moved out. At that point she became Street Cat, moving from one newly parked car to another so she could warm herself against the engines. She was fed by George, a guy who lived a few doors up. His devotion to this friendly mass of knotted fur led his mother to declare, loudly and to the entire street, that her son 'thought too much about pussy'. She also took it upon herself to plant random stuff in the pots outside people's houses, and to water their plants. Once, she tried to give me a pile of Christian literature – she kept it in the shopping trolley she sometimes walked around with – though I wasn't sure if that was because she thought that I was in particular need of saving. After Street Cat had been living rough for twelve years, Peter, who runs the gallery over the road, stepped outside to find her in the gutter – she'd been hit by the street sweeper. It fell upon Peter to break the bad news to George.

The Standard Hotel has been operating since 1865. In the 1980s, when I first moved into the area, the licensee was Handsome Steve Miller, a former member of the Moodists – a band often mentioned in the same breath as the Birthday Party, Laughing Clowns, the Go-Betweens and the Triffids. His collection of country and western paraphernalia still adorns the pub but he took his extensive collection of Geelong Football Club memorabilia (Handsome Steve is a fearsome Cats fan) when he left. These days, he runs a cafe at the Abbotsford Convent called Handsome Steve's House of Refreshment. I miss him. The Standard was the kind of pub you could go to on your own and read the paper by the fire with a whiskey, relying on Steve to keep unwanted admirers – this was when I was young enough to have them – at bay. Then – and now – writers such as Don Watson and Fiona Capp hired rooms above the pub to write in during the day.

In the mid-1980s, the Black Cat cafe in Brunswick Street cultivated a bohemian vibe. Henry Maas, a former performer at Melbourne comedy and cabaret venue the Flying Trapeze and a jazz musician who'd recently returned from Amsterdam, had opened the Black Cat (with Toni and Bruce Edwards) in 1982. As Maas explained, 'Melbourne really needed a place to hang out, so that's what we did, we sort of brought back a bit of Europe'. North of Johnston Street is the slicker Marios, which was opened by Mario Maccarone and Mario DePasquale in 1986. Brunswick Street's social life tended to coalesce around these two poles.

Of course, Europe had been in Brunswick Street for a while before Maas or the Marios arrived. The first cafe and milk bar in the area was Sila, around the corner from our house. It opened in 1959 and still boasts the oldest espresso machine that's been in continuous use in Melbourne. Sila used to be run by Pasquale Zampogna, and since his death it's been run by his son Dominic, who makes extremely good coffee and toasted sandwiches.

Over the summers of 2006 and 2007 I worked at the Brunswick Street Bookstore. My shift was on Sunday nights, from 6 pm until 11 pm. Marios, which is next door, would sometimes extend the waiter service onto the bookstore premises. Massimo – Marios' first employee and an artist – would turn up with our bread basket and white napkins, which we'd have to put to one side while we served customers. Working at the bookstore gave me a perspective on publishing I wish I'd had some years before. It also gave me a strong sense of the rhythm of Brunswick Street. Sudden thunderstorms would turn the street dark, sweep down the tram tracks and drive people into the shop. Heat, on the other hand, would keep them away. Because the shop was air-conditioned you couldn't tell if the temperature had dropped suddenly but you could see the empty street come back to life as people slowly emerged. The hotter the night, the louder the music and the drunker the customers.

Brunswick Street was, and still is if you live and shop in the area, an Italian street. Our now very up-market local greengrocer, the Vegetable Connection, has been run by the Miriklis family since 1941. There's Sila, and, until its closure in 1997, there was the chaotic supermarket-deli-milk bar at 265 Brunswick Street. Apparently a sign on the window once read 'Pizziola Continental and Domestic Groceries', but a year after the shop opened a boy on the street swung at the window with a stick and the shop remained nameless for the rest of its forty-four years. Unrefrigerated cheeses lay piled around the place, interspersed with bulk-buy packs of toilet paper (often displayed in the window) and tins of tomatoes. There was always a queue out the door at lunchtime to buy one of their crusty bread rolls stuffed with huge mortadella and cheese. As journalist Paris Lovett wrote in the *Melbourne Times* in 1997, 'The tall red jars of sun-dried tomatoes and pungent mounds of provolone have long supplied an erotic undercurrent to Fitzroy life'.

Peter and Ida Pizziola provided a bit of an erotic undercurrent themselves. Lovett again:

> Both Peter and Ida grew up on small farms in Treviso, Northern Italy. They met when Peter's sister married Ida's uncle. Peter was twenty-four and Ida was fourteen. Eight months later Peter left

for Australia, and tried unsuccessfully to convince Ida to come with him. He worked in factories, quarries and construction sites, earning £14 a week until he set up the business, with £1600, in 1954. Meanwhile Ida had travelled to England to work as a cook at a Catholic Seminary. Peter wrote letters and sent his sister as emissary, and after twelve years won Ida over. 'I thought, maybe I go to see Australia,' she says. Four days after she arrived they were married, and she joined Peter behind the counter.

The Pizziolas spent their days chatting to customers and giving each other the occasional slap on the bum or a hug, and the memory of their flirtations, after decades of marriage, still brings a smile to my face. When a friend of mine who lived in nearby Moor Street had a child, the couple gave her $100 to buy something because, as they told her, they wished that they'd had one of their own. The Pizziolas almost went broke in the 1960s when the Housing Commission flats were built, but they survived by increasing the wholesale side of the business. According to Lovett: 'This brought an enigmatic aspect to the shop: not only did it offer the continental delicacies that couldn't be found elsewhere, it also stocked Florentine laundry powder, Genovese toothbrushes and Calabrian hammers'.

The Housing Commission flats that scatter the suburb are the result of slum clearances throughout the sixties. At first these clearances were motivated by the social idealism that had sprung up during the Depression in response to the fact that Fitzroy had the highest infant mortality rate in Melbourne. F. Oswald Barnett was born in Brunswick and led campaigns against Melbourne's inner-city slums. In 1936 he was appointed to the Slum Abolition Board, and from 1938 to 1948 he was the vice-chair of the Housing Commission of Victoria. While his survey of southern Fitzroy makes for antiquated reading these days, with much talk of the evils of drink, it's not, perhaps, so different to the articles on the evils of the city's King Street on a Saturday night that became the daily fare of Melbourne's *Herald Sun* and *Age* throughout 2009.

The passion for social reform segued into a love affair with modernism and new technology that lost human dimensions. By the 1960s, Housing Commission houses were replaced by soaring towers, such as those built in Fitzroy's Atherton Estate on the corner of Brunswick and Gertrude streets. As George Cullins wrote in *Fitzroy, Mel-*

bourne's First Suburb, 'When the Atherton Estate was being created in the late 1960s, redevelopment had become a bureaucratic and hectoring procedure aimed at clearing an area and rebuilding as quickly as possible'. This was around the time that Ann Polis, a Fitzroy local whom we still see head off to the gym on her bike every morning, got a group of people together to take over the *Carlton News*. The paper's mission was to fight the Housing Commission's plans to extend high-rise flats across vast tracts of Carlton. It went on to become the *Melbourne Times*, a key chronicler of local political life. The *Carlton News'* first photographer was Tony Knox. He had set up a gift shop, the Poppy Shop, in Lygon Street with his then wife, Pat, before his personal and business partnership with journalist and restaurateur Mietta O'Donnell. I worked at the paper in the mid-eighties, long after Polis had sold it, writing real estate ads and film reviews – in fact I was working at their Rathdowne Street office in March 1986 when the entire terrace shuddered with the force of the bombing of the city's Russell Street police headquarters less than a kilometre away.

Melbourne writer and academic Tony Birch is the author of *Shadowboxing*, a collection of stories about childhood in 1960s Fitzroy. He lived in the last house to be demolished in the now non-existent Atherton Street, and as he recalled in *Fitzroy, Melbourne's First Suburb*:

> Everything was tumbledown and roughly nailed together. But the improvisation worked: it all seemed to hang on. That is, until they bulldozed the lot. My house, my street, and all of the surrounding houses and streets were cleared to make way for high-rise concrete flats. Now there are no houses, no streets, and no landmarks. There are only memories, and some are quite strong.

In 1966, half of Fitzroy's residents were Mediterranean migrants who altered the culture of the suburb. More recent migrants are Asian and African, but these days the isolation of the high-rise Atherton Estate and the pervasive gentrification of the suburb create a greater sense of segregation. But it's also true to say that the towers are a lively place with teenagers playing soccer on the ovals to one side, smaller kids playing with animals at the 'farm' or in the community garden, and chatting parents taking their babies for a walk.

It's easy now to question the building of such huge estates, but there's no question that poverty in the suburb was extreme and the flats were bliss compared to rooming houses in which an entire family would often live in a single room. According to Eleanor Harding, a long-term resident of the towers, 'Lot of them never had a stable home before that, and when they were given a place in what they call "tombstone territory" it was a mansion to them. For the first time they have proper facilities, some privacy and a home of their own.'

Despite intervention, poverty has always had a significant presence in Fitzroy. As the inner city has gone up-market, the cost of housing in Fitzroy has close to doubled in the last five years. It's not uncommon for people to pay close to a million dollars for a tiny terrace. While more extreme in Fitzroy, this is a Melbourne-wide phenomenon. Author Shane Maloney captures the irony of this in his crime novel *The Brush-Off*:

> Laid out by city fathers with Parisian fantasies and strategic interests, Victoria Parade was where the young gentlemen of the Royal Victorian Mounted Volunteers would have drawn their sabres if ever the working-class mob had come storming up the hill from its blighted shacks on the flat below. As it turned out, the tide of history had run

the other way. It was the slums that had fallen, captured by the gentry.

The median price for a house in Melbourne rose from \$463 488 in 2007 to \$540 500 by the end of 2009. Melbourne seemed to be becoming one of the least affordable cities in the world. One explanation for this was the *2030* policy that was attempting to stop Melbourne becoming an endless suburb by including green zones, or green 'wedges' that couldn't be turned into residential developments or freeways. These wedges are terrific for creating a sustainable and varied city environment, but lock up some of the city's real estate, which, some argue, pushes prices up. Whatever the reason, our local real estate agent is quite the celebrity as he walks up and down Brunswick Street in his designer suits or reverse parks one of his luxury cars in front of local cafes. And while I may mock him, he can sell a house that Barnett would have once identified as a slum dwelling for more than a million dollars.

As you walk towards the city you come to Gertrude Street, named after the daughter of early settler Captain Brunswick Smythe. For many years Gertrude Street was home to the Victorian Aboriginal Health Service (established 1973) and other social support services, but in recent years the health service has moved to Nicholson Street and Gertrude is slowly filling with boutiques, bars and restaurants. The gentrification of the street began about twenty years after many other parts of Fitzroy, but it's become rapid, pushing a large number of poorer, often Indigenous, people down to Smith Street. The western end of Gertrude Street near the Carlton Gardens and Nicholson Street is still frequented by a large number of homeless men, many of whom bed down for the night at Osborne House on Nicholson Street – another institution that's survived as a result of FRA intervention in the late seventies. This relocating, formal or otherwise, of our original inhabitants is a constant in Melbourne's history. Meanwhile, Kulin's ceremonial places – such as Rucker's Hill in Northcote, which was once a high point among an area of billabongs – are now sought-after real estate.

Some of the main meeting places for the Aboriginal community in Melbourne in recent years were the parks around Fitzroy and Carlton. They would gather in Atherton Gardens or under one of the large Moreton Bay figs in the Exhibition Gardens. The 'parkies', as they were known, also hung out in small lanes and alleys around Fitzroy. Singer

and songwriter Archie Roach lived on the streets of
Fitzroy for many years and wrote about the experience in 'Charcoal Lane', a song for his first album
of the same name: 'Side by side / We'd walk along
/ to the end of Gertrude St / And we'd tarpaulin
muster / For a quart of wine … In the cold and
in the heat / We'd cross over Smith St / To the end
of the line'.

When Roach was interviewed about that time,
he said:

> If people just saw it on the outside, you know,
> they'd just think, oh, a couple of old Aboriginal
> fellows, or young Aboriginal, couple of Aboriginal
> people drinking in a pack, or whatever, vacant lot,
> vacant area – but it was more than that. That's
> where I learned my history brother, from those
> areas, because all the old fellas, they knew more
> about me than I did, mate.

Charcoal Lane is now the name of a modern Australian restaurant in the bluestone building where
the health centre used to be. It capitalises on the
changes in the street while attempting to stay true
to the area's history – the restaurant trains disad-
vantaged Aboriginal kids and helps them get work
in the food industry. Of the inaugural group of

eighteen trainees, two are from Zimbabwe and the rest are city kids or from the Wurundjeri, Yorta Yorta, Gunditjmara, Kurnai and Boon Wurrung clans.

Once you cross Nicholson Street you're in the European-style Carlton Gardens and the Royal Exhibition Building with its strangely stunted copy of Florence's Duomo (budget cuts meant the building's crowning dome had to be cut in size by a third). The Royal Exhibition Building was built in 1880 because Melbourne, after only forty-five years of existence, was hosting the International Exhibition. In 2004 this beautiful building and its gardens became the first urban site in Australia to be given World Heritage status. The gardens are an important part of that listing, though in autumn 2009 if you had crossed the park and headed for Rathdowne Street you would have walked through an avenue of distressed and dying poplars, oaks and elms. Orange plastic water wells had been scattered around the park, dripping recycled water directly to roots in an attempt to save them from drought that both starves the trees of water and makes them more vulnerable to being blown over during the city's increasingly violent storms. This was happening all over Melbourne, and the city council was beginning to remove dying trees and replace them with more drought-resistant species. Tree planting began in Birdwood Avenue near the Shrine of Remembrance, where lemon-scented gum trees replaced the Lombardy poplars. The oaks along Alexandra Avenue close to the Yarra River would soon be replaced as well.

After the gardens, you walk another kilometre or so down Queensberry Street and you're at Queen Victoria Market. Melbourne exists in part because of its markets – managing them was the reason for the establishment of the Melbourne City Council in 1842. While Queen Victoria Market is the oldest, there are significant markets in South Melbourne, Dandenong and Prahran. When I was a kid the Prahran Market was my family's market of choice and the highlight for me was the Car Park Man. Even today I half expect to see a man standing on a precarious steel tower with a megaphone, directing cars. Instead there is now a covered car park, complete with ticket machines, one of which has the following sign scrawled onto a bit of paper and taped to the side of it: 'If paying by Cridet Card Mastercard or visa only'.

Once I became a student, and was living northside, I frequented Queen Victoria Market. When

I moved to Sydney, the Queen Vic was – unexpectedly – the place in Melbourne that I missed without reservation. One of the first things I did on my return was shop there. Nine months later I began going, every Saturday morning, with Virginia. We're going together still. The experience is as much a visual feast as anything: there are piles of red chillies, orange mangoes, bright lemons, pale balls of buffalo mozzarella, the pink of uncooked salmon. And the greens: parsley, cucumber, basil, rocket, spring onions, lettuces and beans. But it's not just the eyes that feast. There is, inevitably, a bratwurst with way too much sauerkraut to be eaten, or a jam donut to be devoured. Julie Boening's family has been selling donuts from the caravan on Berkeley Street inside the market for more than fifty years and over two generations. And bloody good they are too – it's almost impossible to resist those freshly made hot sugary balls of jam. She told *The Age*:

> The market community is probably not as close-knit as it used to be, but the wonderful atmosphere, the hustle and bustle, has stayed the same … I feel a real sense of belonging to the Victoria Market. I grew up here really and have been coming here almost every week of my life.

Markets have been operating in the areas between Queen and Elizabeth streets since 1857. At first there was a livestock market, then a meat market, and by 1878 a fruit and vegetable market was there as well. To accommodate the expansion, forty-five bodies buried on the grounds were exhumed and reburied in Carlton's Melbourne General Cemetery: much of today's market is built on Melbourne's first formal cemetery. The brown and cream wall that runs through the centre of the market is, in fact, the old cemetery wall. When the market expanded again in 1920 all identifiable graves in the area were exhumed but the unmarked graves were left alone. These unmarked graves included many of the area's Aboriginal inhabitants, including resistance fighters Robert Smallboy and Jack Napoleon Tunermenerwail. In 1842 Smallboy and Tunermenerwail were the first people to be formally executed in Melbourne, having led a guerilla campaign against white settlers who had moved to Bass River. In 1930 Melbourne's tabloid *Truth* ran the headline 'Remains of Early Settlers Tossed Callously Aside to Rot in Mud' after a pile of bones was discovered during another round of renovations – and promptly dumped in the North Melbourne tip. An investigation into overcrowded market conditions in 1948 ordered for the whole-sale market to be transferred to Footscray Road. This didn't eventuate until 1969, after which there was a decade-long battle to stave off the closure of the retail market altogether and build a shopping complex in its place. This battle, fought by the Builders Labourers Federation and community groups, eventually saved the market and resulted in it being classified by the National Trust and listed as a historic place by Heritage Victoria.

Inevitably, given the range of small businesses, the cash economy and the money to be made, our markets aren't all jam donuts and perfect cheeses: they have, at times, been the centre of criminal activity. In 1963 and 1964 there was a series of murders at Queen Victoria Market, the first of which was the shooting of Vincenzo Angilletta in April 1963. Several deaths later, on 31 January 1964, *Time* magazine reported the struggle for supremacy over the market: 'As Melbourne last week was shaken by the shotgun explosions of gang warfare, Australians became aware that the new Italian immigrants had also brought with them the blood feuds of the Mafia and Camorra, as well as the code of silence induced by omerta (death for informers)'. The article noted that trading at the market was done almost entirely in cash and that an estimated $45 million worth of fruit and vegetables passed through each year. Back in 1964, that was a lot of money. The FBI sent out their top organised crime expert, the fabulously named (if you're a Generation X-er) John Cusack. His report on the market extortion racket was ignored for years, probably as a result of corruption within the Victorian police force at that time.

The relationship between the markets and organised crime began in the 1930s, with the arrival from Italy of one Domenico Italiano. He established the Melbourne arm of the Honoured Society, a Calabrian 'Ndrangheta criminal organisation. Italiano encouraged people from Italy to move to Victoria and set up market gardens here. As a result, according to investigative journalist and author of several books on Australian organised crime Bob Bottom:

> Italiano and his associates took over control of
> those supplying the markets. Other Italians ended
> up virtual slaves. They had to repay the money
> that was used to bring them out. Whether they
> grew the produce or they sold it through the
> markets, they all paid tribute. Growers or sellers
> at the markets weren't always aware of the full

background of who they were dealing with or how the system worked.

Italiano died (of natural causes, in bed) in 1962 and was replaced by Liborio Benvenuto. Around this time Angilletta had, unwisely, started a group called La Bastarda in opposition to the Honoured Society. It was Benvenuto who allegedly ordered Angilletta's murder and those that followed. Benvenuto remained Godfather until he was 88. He died, as Italiano had before him, of natural causes and from his deathbed asked his son-in-law, Alfonso Muratore (son of Vincent, one of the victims of the Market Murders twenty-eight before), to lead the Honoured Society. This effectively ousted his son, Frank. Alfonso declined and soon after left Angela Benvenuto for his mistress, Karen Mansfield. As a consequence he was forced out of Footscray's Wholesale Fruit and Vegetable Market, where he worked. Frank Benvenuto took over his stand. Alfonso signed his death warrant four years later when he offered cheaper rates to senior buyers at Coles Myer than those they were getting through the Honoured Society. He was gunned down two weeks later by, it is presumed, Frank Benvenuto.

Though Alfonso Muratore's death was not officially part of what's now known as the gangland murders, there is no doubt that the younger generation of organised criminals have not had the luxury of anointing future leaders from their deathbeds. Between 1998 and 2009 there were 34 gangland-related murders. Frank Benvenuto, who was rumoured to have become a police informant and suspected of alerting detectives to corruption in the Wholesale Fruit and Vegetable Market, died in 2000. He was shot in the chest in daylight as he sat at the wheel of his Holden outside his Beaumaris home.

Early in autumn 2009 I had lunch with a friend I've been close to since we went to Monash University together. Deb Verhoeven is a film and television critic, and we met to eat at a place called East Imperial that did good yum cha. Back in 2004 the restaurant had been called La Porcella and served Italian food, becoming notorious as the place where Andrew Veniamin, an associate of Frank Benvenuto and later a chief suspect in his killing, was gunned down. Mick Gatto was later acquitted of Veniamin's murder on the grounds of self-defence. Gatto too was a child of the markets, as he described in his autobiography, *I, Gatto*:

> My mother and father were both immigrants
> from Calabria in the south of Italy. My father was

one of the first Italians to settle in the country, coming over in the 1920s ... In the 1950s he got involved in the markets in Melbourne, where he worked for more than 50 years – the rest of his life. First he was at the Footscray Wholesale Market, and then he had his own stall at the South Melbourne Market ... I used to get to the wholesale market at four or five in the morning. I'd work in the retail market two or three days a week until perhaps 5 pm. And I'd have every night off.

Deb joked, as only a Melburnian could, that you know Andrew Veniamin is about to die in the eleventh episode of the gangland television series *Underbelly* when he orders an emasculating *weak* cappuccino. 'The thing about crime stories', Deb said, 'is particularity. It doesn't work if people are driving down a generic street. They need to be turning left from Fitzroy Street onto the Esplanade.' Or, to quote an early episode of *Homicide*, 'On Lygon Street, Carlton, heading north'. We went on to discuss other examples of the particularity of geography in crime drama. Shane Maloney's Murray Whelan novels are set in and around Melbourne's Brunswick, Michael Connelly's Harry

Bosch is from Los Angeles, and Ian Rankin's Rebus hails from Edinburgh. We talked for a bit about Melbourne television and the penchant for crime series, from *Consider Your Verdict* (1961–63) through *Homicide* (1964–77) and *Division 4* (1969–75) to the contemporary *Underbelly*.

As a kid I loved both *Homicide* (the first episode of which was set at the University of Melbourne) and *Division 4*. I loved seeing my small, flat hometown on the screen of our wood veneer TV. Moments of recognition like this had disappeared by the 1980s when most television production had moved to Sydney and you certainly weren't likely to 'come across a *Homicide* film unit anywhere in Melbourne, at any time of the day or night', as newspaper ads warned you might back in 1964. There has been a shift back again, however, and series such as *City Homicide* and *Rush* are now produced out of Melbourne.

As we were eating our final dumplings, Deb showed me a cartoon from 1929 in which 'John Melbourne' imagines Sydneysiders bodysurfing at Bondi and 'John Sydney' imagines Melburnians lurking with their guns tucked into their raincoats, much as Squizzy Taylor, Melbourne's most notorious gangster back then, might have done.

Taylor started working for John Wren in 1916 and morphed into a particularly stylish – and violent – gangster who was involved in the Fitzroy Vendetta of 1919, in which rival racketeers fought for territory. He ran a protection racket and dealt in, among other illegal things, prostitution and cocaine. He died of gunshot wounds – inflicted by a standover man from Sydney – in Fitzroy's St Vincent Hospital in 1927.

April's sweet moderation was particularly welcome in 2009. The nights cooled, the days were sunny and mild, and we woke, as we do each year, to the whoosh of hot air balloons as blasts of gas buoy them ever higher. The balloons take off from Royal Park – Burke and Wills' departure point back in 1860 as they set off towards the Gulf of Carpentaria – and float above the city, luminous in the dawn light. Our mornings usually involve exercise: early enough to catch a glimpse of the new moon rising, the time on the Fitzroy Town Hall's illuminated clock and, occasionally, the rising sun. I head off to the Gertrude Street Yoga Studio at 6.30 am, where a group of us sit in a large room in what used to be Johnston's Department Store. The room has a glass-domed light well that threatens to collapse at any moment, and the walls are made convex by age, not design. There is a vacant lot below the window where birds chatter as they wake. Dressed in daggy tracksuits, we listen to the early trams go by as we salute the sun, make like warriors and do the plank. Around the same time, Virginia and several friends head to the Carlton Gardens to torture themselves at boot camp.

April is also bat time of year, and the huge gum tree in the courtyard of the gallery across the road from our house is home to roosting fruit bats for most of the month and into May. For a month or so, you go to sleep listening to the sound of their screeching. A few years ago there was talk of culling the colony of 5000 bats – a number that swells to 20 000 at some times of the year – living in Melbourne's Royal Botanic Gardens. There were protests against the idea of poisoning them, given that this was the only breeding colony of flying foxes in Victoria and the southern-most colony in the world. In the end the bats were driven out of the gardens by high frequencies of noise, and these days they roost in Fairfield Park.

Both the bats and the Royal Botanic Gardens

were memorialised in Shane Maloney's *The Brush-Off*, when the novel's hapless hero, Murray Whelan, is interrupted by bat activity late one night:

> Melbourne's Botanic Gardens are approximately the size of Uganda. At the best of times, finding your way out takes a compass, a ball of twine, and access to satellite navigation ... Here and there we stopped, pressed against each other in beds of flowering succulents, stamen brushing pistil, inhaling nectar. Pissed to the eyeballs. My fingers were sticky with liquidambar. My aching prick was as hard and smooth as the trunk of the ghost gum, *Eucalyptus papuana*, planted here by Viscount de Lisle, Governor-General of Australia, 1961-65.

Where the gardens now stand was once wet-lands that extended across to the other side of the Yarra — then a narrower river — to what is now the Jolimont rail yards. These wetlands were one of the areas where the Wurundjeri fished for eel (though billabongs up around what is now Bulleen were also a favoured spot). It was in these wetlands, in early 1839, when the settlement was less than five years old, that some Kulin gathered in a camp to make up a welcoming party for the newly arrived Chief Protector of Aborigines, George Augustus

Robinson. The wetlands were drained by Charles La Trobe in 1846 so the gardens could be developed, though there are some large eucalypts that pre-date the gardens' establishment. One such tree is the prominent Separation Tree, a 300-year-old river red gum under which Victoria was declared a separate colony in 1855. (That tree was ringbarked by vandals in August 2010. It's not yet clear if it will survive.)

William Guilfoyle, the gardens' second director, undertook the landscaping that formed the lovely, slightly eccentric, gardens we know today. His ideas were influenced by the landscapes and geographical features he had seen while on a scientific expedition in the South Sea Islands in 1868, which explains, in part, the gardens' most famous folly: Guilfoyle's Volcano. Unlike most follies, the volcano's purpose was partly practical in that it stored and circulated water. Melbourne didn't have piped water until the completion of the Yan Yean reservoir in 1857, and even then it was many years before supply was consistent. There were problems to overcome, such as the massive 1878 floods that destroyed the bridge that carried the Yan Yean aqueduct over the Plenty River.

The volcano, placed at the highest point of

the gardens, acted as both a water catchment and an irrigation feed for the gardens — and it's been restored to that purpose today. In recent years the gardens' management have had to do an enormous amount of work with water conservation. *Floreo*, the Royal Botanic Gardens magazine, describes the shift:

> The effects of climate change have seen the end of the long era of gardening in this dry continent when, in the words of garden historian Paul Fox, technology was used to 'water foreign plants to create the successful myth of Australia as a garden oasis reminiscent of foreign places.'

One of the results of the early approach to gardens that Fox mentions is that most of the Royal Botanic Gardens' species were non-native, and as a consequence the gardens effectively introduced many intrusive species. These days they are home to more than 50 000 individual species, and while many of them are still non-native there is an increasing emphasis on plants that grow well in arid conditions. The days of the faux South Sea Islands and lush grottos I loved as a child are almost gone.

After morning exercise Virginia and I would often head to Newtown S.C., a cafe in Brunswick Street named after the social club that originally existed at its address – Newtown being a former name for the southern end of Fitzroy. The then owner of Newtown S.C., Cate Della Bosca, is a passionate Hawthorn supporter and her customers enjoyed the banter over the weekend's footy results as much as they did the coffee. An impressive tipping competition took up a large section of the cafe wall. Photos of Hawthorn's Chance Bateman, dreadlocks flying out behind him, were displayed next to the postcards customers had sent Cate from around the world – the kitschier the better.

One Saturday morning, Cate looked particularly sad. Hawthorn had been thrashed by Essendon at the Melbourne Cricket Ground the night before, and after the game Cate had ridden her bike home in the rain. 'It's hard to describe how pathetic you can feel riding a bike home on a wet night after your football team has lost', she said to me. She's right. There should be a word for this very particular state of angst.

Sure, you could argue that any sport is a highly emotional business, but in Melbourne it is the Australian Football League that's responsible for the city's particular moodiness: the tension, the near wins, the exhilaration of expected losses unexpectedly turning victorious. Football captures something about the absurdity of life, the tricky combination of hard work and luck that reduces barrackers to a kind of superstitious fatalism. A game, and a club's history, can turn on small moments of courage, maybe on some intelligent coaching, and on things as ephemeral as the weather and the state of a player's, or indeed the coach's, marriage.

In footy academic Matthew Klugman's description of the phenomenon, the game:

> produces suffering and joy, and an insatiable
> hunger for more … Mad, fevered, obsessed,
> fanatical, addicted. These are just a few of the
> words routinely invoked to describe Aussie Rules
> barrackers by critics *and* fans. It's as if the strange
> passions of footy followers are pathological. And
> perhaps they are.

It's not surprising, really, that John Wren died a month after suffering a heart attack watching his team, Collingwood, win the 1953 grand final. A close game can do that to you.

When Sydney-based journalist Mark Dapin

asked me to describe what Melbourne's love affair with football was about, I commented that 'It's kind of an induction into a cult'. If I'd been quicker on my literary feet, I would've quoted Albert Camus at him, as Melbourne writer Tim Richards once did to me:

> Camus says that we need to imagine that Sisyphus will find a way to rethink his curse in a way that permits happiness. We football fans need to imagine that the number 5 in our colours has our emotional well being in mind as he lines up the goals. That he cares about us as much as he cares about himself.

I commissioned approximately 200 essays during my term at *Meanjin*, on topics as various as government funding bodies, cartooning, the death of a young child, skateboarding, copyright laws, new media, religion, theatre and art. Yet the single most contentious article I published in the journal was by Ciannon Cazaly — yes, she's related to the famous player Roy Cazaly — on the culture wars surrounding discussion of football's origins. Many argue, Cazaly included, that the game grew out of an indigenous game called Marngrook. Certainly that game involved high leaping, a unique characteristic of Australian Rules, and the kicking around of a possum-skin ball not dissimilar to the kind used in the contemporary game. Some historians claim there is little evidence of this, while others argue that such claims are a way of denying Melbourne's European immigrants their legacy as bearers of the game of soccer to our lands. What is not in doubt is that many of the league's best players are, and have been, Indigenous.

The first season of the Victorian Football League was played in 1897 with eight clubs: Carlton, Collingwood, Essendon, Fitzroy, Geelong, Melbourne, St Kilda and South Melbourne. In 1908, Richmond and University joined them. In 1914, University merged with Melbourne. In 1925, Footscray, North Melbourne and Hawthorn joined the league. This list of twelve teams remained unchanged for fifty-seven years. Until the mid-eighties, the VFL residency rules meant that players lived and worked in their team's suburb (or its catchment area). They weren't just blokes you saw playing on the ground, you bumped into them at the pub! At the petrol station! At the milk bar! Working hours also allowed for greater participation in supporting the local team. In the early 20th century, Richmond's Pelaco factory closed on Saturdays in time for women to get the game. In fact, a canopy had to be constructed over the Richmond players' entry onto the field because women, angry at some of the performances, were poking them with knitting needles. There is a long tradition of Richmond fans actively haranguing their team.

In 1982 South Melbourne was struggling financially. Its home suburb had changed demographically and the team was left with a small supporter base. Increasingly, many Melbourne teams were facing this problem. The VFL board decided to move the South Melbourne Swans to Sydney. In 1985, the board opened the way for private ownership of teams by selling the Swans to Dr Geoffrey Edelsten, a 'medical entrepreneur' (and later prison inmate, following a conviction for soliciting an underworld figure to assault a former patient). In 1987, a new team was created in Brisbane and was briefly owned by another bankrupt in the making, Christopher Skase. Perth's West Coast Eagles – a particularly impressive side that has won three premierships – also joined that year. Not surprisingly, both clubs with private owners got into strife and were forced to revert to more traditional membership-based financial structures. In 1990 the Adelaide Crows joined the league and in 1995 the Fremantle Dockers from Western Australia got on board. In 1996 the Brisbane Bears merged with Melbourne-based Fitzroy to become the Brisbane Lions; the last player from the Fitzroy days, Chris Johnson, played his final game in 2007. The most recent addition to the AFL was Port Adelaide in 1997.

Many feared that broadening the league from a Victorian-based organisation to a national one would hasten the demise of the community spirit that has defined Melbourne since the late 1890s. While that worst-case scenario has not come to pass, there is no doubt that the years in which the premiership cup has been held interstate (1992, 1994, 1997, 1998 and, tragically, 2001–2006) have been flat ones. As a consequence the city was almost uniformly united in its support of Geelong in the 2007 grand final because there was a chance a Victorian team might win the flag for the first time since 2000. They did.

It's not uncommon for three or four generations of a family to follow one team. Fathers and sons, in particular, are bonded by the game, a subject James Button wrote about very movingly after the death of his father in 2008. John Button was a politician and he was also a significant supporter of and fundraiser for the Geelong Football Club. While he was known throughout Australia as the Minister for Industry and Commerce under prime ministers Bob Hawke and Paul Keating, in Melbourne it was his allegiance to football that was as often discussed. According to James:

> The only other place I saw my dad really let himself go was at the football. He was seriously, battily, obsessed by football, and by the Geelong Football Club. More than once, in the Geelong changing rooms, I caught Dad staring a little too intently at Gary Ablett's thighs. Week after week, year on year, he would draw an oval on a sheet of paper and compile his team in his crimped handwriting, which a secretary of his once compared to the scratchings of a chook. Sometimes he would mail them to the coach; always he would mail them to Nick and me. I think football was a great release from politics. More than that, though, it gave him a chance to be with his two sons, and I know that his love of football was also a love of us.

My relationship with the game is both by marriage – Virginia's love of football is such that if we were to ever move away from Melbourne, it would be as if a major artery had been severed – and familial. When I was a child my dad used to take my brother and me to watch Carlton play at Princes Park. My most vivid memory of those years is of my three-year-old brother, Saul, strapped into a baby car seat that was then tied to the wire fence at the back of the outer so he could get a good view. Dad went to the footy with a group of Carlton friends, including the playwright Jack Hibberd and other La Mama and Pram Factory identities. Actor Graeme Blundell later described the ritual:

> There was a charm and modesty about La Mama, and a kind of purposeful impermanence that resisted institutionalisation. Just as there was at the 'Outer', at our beloved Princes Park where a group of actors and writers from La Mama would troop through the damp grass and fallen elm leaves to join in our cohorts whenever the Carlton football team played at home. The Outer was like a sacred site for us...

There was a reason why my dad, who was Brisbane born, loved Carlton so. Soon after he arrived in Melbourne, the team played in the most famous grand finals of modern history: the 1970 Collingwood–Carlton match. 'The 1970 grand final is a Melbourne story. Couldn't 'ave happened anywhere else', said Bert Thornley, a player for Carlton, who was interviewed by Martin Flanagan for his book on the match, *1970 and Other Stories of the Australian Game*. At the time the game was moving away from the traditional model, a model in which footballers were ordinary blokes who fitted football in around their work as gardeners, real estate agents, teachers and labourers. This shift was a problem for Collingwood because, as a working-class club, they paid all their players the same wage. Carlton, on the other hand, was developing flexible pay scales. Either way, the money didn't compare to wages these days, when the minimum a footballer earns is $49 400 plus $2800 per senior match, while the best players are on half a million or more. Modern players are superstars of sorts, whether they want to be or not – a pressure that has driven many good players out of the game.

Collingwood and Carlton were – and, along with Essendon, still are – Melbourne's biggest clubs. Collingwood formed back in 1890. Its colours are black and white, and so are the emotions the club provokes: devotion and antipathy. In 1970 Carlton was arguably still a working-class suburb with a high proportion of Mediterranean migrants. As in Fitzroy, the Housing Commission was committed to tearing a lot of the suburb down and rebuilding it. Carlton players who were on ground in the 1970 final included the Italian Sergio Silvagni; the Ukrainian-Russian Alex Jesaulenko; and the then only Aboriginal player in the league, Syd Jackson. Robert Walls, a younger player on the team, is now a footy columnist for *The Age*. Percy Jones is now known as the proprietor of Percy's, a pub on the corner of Elgin and Lygon streets in Carlton. Young Teddy Hopkins kicked four inspirational goals to ensure Carlton's win that day, but soon chucked it all in to become a poet. But the real star of the team was Brent Crosswell, often thought to be the inspiration for the stoned footy player in David Williamson's play *The Club*. Crosswell was considered to be an 'intellectual', whatever that meant, and was certainly a self-confessed smoker of marijuana. I met him once, when I was nine or so, because my mum taught him Politics at night school. Young as I was, I could see he had charisma. He never appeared to take the game that seriously. Despite, or because of, his ambivalence, he was totally unpredictable. And when he was at his best, he was brilliant.

In 1970 Collingwood's coach was the legendary Bobby Rose (father of Peter Rose, editor of the *Australian Book Review*). He was a brilliant footballer in his time and a good coach. But Carlton's Ron Barassi was something else. Barassi brought with him what Flanagan has called a 'corporate conservatism'. This meant many things, including rigorous fitness, the banning of beards and regulations on hair length. It's been argued that Barassi invented the 'modern' style of play during the 1970 final itself.

There were 122 000 people attending the game at the MCG – the biggest crowd it's ever held. Carlton trailed at half-time by 44 points, which caused Barassi to alternately berate his players (upending a table in the club rooms, reminding them how humiliating a loss to Collingwood would feel) and rouse them (to win without risk is to triumph without glory!). He also exhorted them to use more hand passes, and that instruction was part of the evolution into the game we're watching forty years later: a more fluid and dynamic one in which players run further and are less bound by the positions they're officially placed in.

After half-time Carlton began to dominate. Finally, twenty-five minutes into the final quarter, after a goal kicked by Crosswell, they led by four points. They went on to win by ten.

The 1970 grand final is also the game in which Alex Jesaulenko took one of the 20th century's greatest marks – though you'd have to say that title would have been contested by a couple of Gary Ablett's for Geelong in the early nineties. Certainly the image of Jezza lifting himself off Graeme (Jerker) Jenkin's shoulders to take the ball is one of the most iconic in football, as is the commentary by Mike Williamson, who shouted, 'Oh Jesaulenko, you beauty!' The moment even had a song written about it: TISM's 'The Back Upon Which Jezza Jumped'. That mark was certainly the point at which Jezza became a star, and my brother remembers going to the loo at half-time during games in the seventies only to hear a bunch of blokes singing, 'Jesaulenko walks on water'. Religion and footy are never far apart.

Melbourne has always been a funny town. Even the meanest (and consequently most famous) quote about the place was written, by a local, as a joke. Actress Ava Gardner never did say '*On the Beach* is a story about the end of the world, and Melbourne sure is the right place to film it'. A young journalist who was working on Sydney's *Sun-Herald* in 1959 made the quote up. Neil Jillett's story had been a bit of a struggle to write, it seems, because Miss Gardner was more focused on cocktails than interviews, so for a laugh he wrote the following as the final paragraph of his story, never intending it to run:

> It has not been confirmed that Miss Gardner, as has been rumoured at third hand from a usually unreliable source, if given the chance, would seriously consider whether, if she managed to think of it, would like to have put on the record that she said: '*On the Beach* is a story about the end of the world, and Melbourne sure is the right place to film it.'

Instead of checking the paragraph with Jillett, the subs just assumed it was another example of a reporter who couldn't write, cleaned up the copy and sent it to print. Despite Jillett's attempts over the years to correct the record, the myth lives on. And while Melbourne is a town that takes itself seriously, it also takes seriously the art of shitcanning people who take themselves seriously. Consequently, the absurd yet highly particular passions AFL provoke provide much comic material.

The tragedy of comedian Dave Hughes's devotion to Carlton certainly enlivens the television show *Before the Game*, while the Sydney-based team of Roy and HG (aka John Doyle and Greig Pickhaver) wrung philosophy from footy with their show on radio station triple j (*This Sporting Life*, from 1986 to 2008) and continue to do so on Triple M. Few Melburnians will have forgotten the entertainment before a grand final in the late nineties where a group of young kids in their trackie dacks performed a choreographed routine around maypoles. The scene was beyond ridiculous, but HG transported it into brilliance when he pronounced, 'Here we have a symbol of Howard's relaxed and comfortable Australia'.

The Coodabeen Champions have raised parochialism to an art form since they first aired on Melbourne community radio station 3RRR (Triple R) in 1981; their show, now on ABC Local Radio, has provided the soundtrack to my winter Saturdays for the last thirty years. The makeup of the group tells you a lot about how deeply rooted football culture is in Melbourne. Its current members are academic Jeff Richardson, former journalist Ian Cover, singer

Greg Champion, singer Billy Baxter and teacher Torch McGee. Former members of the group include footy commentator Tony Leonard, and Simon Whelan, now a Judge of the Supreme Court of Victoria. One of the reasons the Coodabeens have been so successful is that their formula has barely changed. Various segments include 'Covie's Quiz', a football-related quiz run by Ian Cover; 'Guru Bob', the Coodabeens' special adviser on football spirituality; Greg Champion's songs that play endlessly with the class stereotypes associated with football; and 'Torch's Footy Talkback', a talk radio segment where fictional callers phone in with various football questions or general musings on life. Class mockery is at the heart of much of the humour. Skiing Volvo drivers barrack for the Dees (Melbourne), latte-drinking wankers with kids in private school barrack for Hawthorn, and Melbourne Uni student Nigel from North Fitzroy barracks for Fremantle 'to be ironic'. There are moments when this satire rings scarily true. When Virginia and I bought a Volvo hatchback, the car came complete with a Melbourne cap and information on where to buy good snow chains. The city was, and is still in some ways, a network of warring winter tribes — each tribe absurd in its own special way.

The most moving – and yes, I use that word mindfully – segment of the show is usually 'Outer Barcoo', which profiles regional amateur or semi-professional football teams and features interviews with players and coaches. Footy is essential to community in country Victoria, as indeed it was in Melbourne before the shift from the VFL to the AFL. After the Black Saturday fires, footballers were among the first to visit Kinglake, and it was only eight weeks after fire destroyed their town that the Kinglake football team played their first game of the season.

These days Melbourne is so officially funny that the Melbourne International Comedy Festival, established by John Pinder in 1987, generates a turnover of over $10 million a year and has over 1760 performers in more than 300 separate shows. In 2010 the festival's general manager, Virginia Lovett, put out a statement saying, 'With the ongoing support of the government and corporate supporters the Melbourne International Comedy Festival will continue to be a major cultural tourism destination in Autumn as well as providing a hub for performers [*sic*] development'.

According to Shane Maloney, who was the festival's general manager in the early days, the original intent was to recognise 'an existing reservoir of absurdity and playfulness' in the wider Melbourne community. In an interview with Lorin Clarke for an article on the festival commissioned by *Meanjin*, Maloney went on to say 'the idea behind the festival wasn't to generate shows with "people in Melbourne watching people telling them jokes"; it was instead a conceptual umbrella erected over the city "giving people a licence to be silly"'.

The festival's launch on April Fools' Day 1987 involved the wider Melbourne community. Clarke writes: 'The *Age* released a fake front page. The chief magistrate opened his court for a mock trial involving local performers and members of the public. The festival hired two men to wander around Melbourne dressed as Melbourne City Council workers and scavenge in rubbish bins for food.'

Four years later there was an opening gala; Celebrity Theatresports, where comedian Tony Martin made his only Theatresports appearance 'to little effect'; and the 2nd Annual Comedy Festival Debate where, according to Martin, 'the topic was, as I think it was every year for a while, "That

Sydney is funnier than Melbourne" (Bob Ellis and David Williamson argued "for". I don't think there was time for a rebuttal)'. Martin notes that the Athenaeum Theatre was home to *Homicide Live*, 'a staged version of the Crawfords TV classic with, what the ad claims is, "the original cast", but I note that none are named', while John Clarke and Ross Stevenson's *A Royal Commission into the Australian Economy*, directed by the late Frank Gallagher, 'remains the funniest show ever written about that subject'.

All this is a far cry from the focus on stand-up comedy that characterises the festival today. The shift occurred, Clarke argues, in the nineties during the reign of Jeff Kennett as the state's premier:

> The festival's fight for financial survival has compromised its pursuit of that original aim of encouraging communal cheek … In 1994 Susan Provan was appointed festival director. Maloney remembers the precarious position the festival was in due to government pressure on arts organisations in Victoria at the time of Provan's appointment. For all its inventiveness and inspiration, the festival needed management that answered to the government's 'obsession with economic viability'.

When I first lived in Fitzroy, the Last Laugh Theatre, Restaurant and Zoo, owned by John Pinder, was a favourite haunt. It sat on the corner of Smith and Gertrude streets (before its incarnation as a comedy venue it was an unemployment office; nowadays it's A Bar Called Barry) and is an example of how much difference just one building, one venue, can make to the cultural life of a city. In 1986, comedian Wendy Harmer described her initial attraction to the burgeoning scene:

> While doing the occasional theatre reviews for the *Melbourne Times* and the *National Times* about five years ago, the door opened for me on the wonderful world of Melbourne Cabaret – Los Trios Ringbarkus at the Flying Trapeze Cafe, Quantock and Kenneally at the Comedy Cafe, Circus Oz and the Whittles at the Last Laugh. It was extraordinary, mesmerising.

I was lucky enough to see Judith Lucy in one of her first public performances back in the mid-eighties at La Joke, the small room above the larger cabaret space at the Last Laugh. She was making jokes about being a waitress at the vegetarian restaurant up the street, Soul Food. As a consequence, for 25 years I've imagined Judith as a waitress who works down the road from my house – only recently it finally dawned on me that she is really quite famous. This overfamiliarity is in itself quite a Melbourne phenomenon, and a reason why people – not just comics – need to leave the place from time to time.

In the seventies Melbourne's comedy scene was explicitly political, continuing the work of performers like Max Gillies, who began at the Pram Factory, and Mary Kenneally and Evelyn Krape, who cut their teeth in feminist revues. Circus Oz, while more cabaret than comedy, emerged in 1977 and had particularly coherent feminist politics. As an article in *The Age* noted, Circus Oz was formed

> with a mandate to be not just an entertaining force, but a political one. Over the years, the company has raised nearly $250 000 for refugees and asylum seekers, performed at the Villawood Detention Centre, consciously staffed an equal number of women and men, and featured gags highlighting everything from the Vietnam War to uranium mining.

Circus Oz co-founder Tim Coldwell – best known for his 32-year performance of a man getting up and going to work while suspended upside down from the ceiling of the tent – told *The Age* that 'people think [feminism's] all happened, and everybody's the same, but when you look at it, still women get paid less than men, women don't get the jobs, don't have as much power [as men]. It's a point that constantly needs to be hammered, otherwise it goes backwards.'

These days the local comedy scene is far more commodified than it once was, making it arguably less political. The Comedy Festival has set up programs to encourage diversity and community contribution, which has helped. One Comedy Festival founder and regular who has not changed his act, Rod Quantock said recently, 'The festival destroyed live comedy in Melbourne to a great degree'. Quantock was a writer and performer in the 1969 Melbourne University Architects Revue and has been performing political comedy ever since. He's appeared on or been otherwise involved in most of the comedy television shows of the last three decades, including *Australia You're Standing in It*, *Fast Forward*, *Denton*, *The Big Gig* and *Good News Week*. Most famously he takes his audiences on bus tours, flourishing a rubber chicken on the end of a stick. They visit Melbourne institutions like the Melbourne Club, while the entire tour group wears

Groucho Marx noses, moustaches and glasses. His 2009 festival show, 'Bugger the Polar Bears: This is Serious', was about climate change. When promoting it he said, 'I'm never going to be a regular guest on the new *Hey Hey it's Saturday* for instance. I've been pigeon-holed as that left wing loony comedian.' This is a shame, as it would have been both amusing and informative to watch Quantock's response to the infamous skit on the *Hey Hey* reunion in October 2009. Men in blackface performed 'the Jackson Jive', re-enacting a Red Faces talent segment from 1989. One of the judges, American singer Harry Connick Jr, gave them zero, saying, 'If they turned up looking like that in the United States, it would be like "hey, hey, there's no more show"'.

It's surprising to realise that 3.15 million viewers (the majority of the show's viewers always have been, and always will be, from Melbourne) were watching that night, which meant that *Hey Hey* was renewed for a season in 2010. When *Hey Hey* began, early one Saturday morning in 1971, my brother and I were in raptures. We loved Ossie Ostrich, the puppet played by Ernie Carroll, a former writer for comedy legend Graham Kennedy. The show was playful and chaotic – exuberant in its celebration of its vaudeville roots. But we grew up and the show didn't. Instead it became an iconic example of what Mark Davis describes as 'the way Australian culture remains stuck in the 1970s, reliant on backwards-looking aesthetics and modes of understanding, unwilling to add new voices and ideas to mainstream discussion'. It's a holding on to the past that was glorified in the years that John Howard was prime minister, and so deeply has this particular example of recidivism become embedded in Melbourne's psyche that it's became a real flashpoint for cultural tensions. Having criticised *Hey Hey*'s renewal in her television column for *The Age*'s *Green Guide,* Marieke Hardy received some unpleasant reader feedback:

> More than one person suggested that the reason I didn't like *Hey Hey* was because I had a 'foreign' name and should go back to where I came from … There was certainly a sense of 'those fancy-pants, latte-sipping socialists wouldn't know real Aussie humour' with the more rabid fans. It's astonishing to think that simply suggesting a show might have had its day could be seen as thumbing the nose at an entire demographic.

Comedy is, of course, entirely based on thumbing

one's nose. And if it can be harder to find in the pubs of Melbourne these days, it can be found online if you look for the work of – among others – Lou Sanz, Justin Heazlewood and Anne Edmonds or follow tweeters like @andrewbolt, who is in fact a parody of the conservative commentator.

Melbourne's comedy scene, though, has middle-class rather than humble beginnings. It was born in a middle-class suburb: Camberwell, to be exact, and its mother was Mrs Louisa Humphries. According to Graeme Blundell, comedian Barry Humphries

> tells of returning from a wonderful afternoon
> tea at the house of one of his mother's friends
> and remarking on how much he enjoyed the
> cake they'd been served. His mother's one-word
> response sums up much of the class snobbery that
> he would spend his life dissecting. 'Bought!' she
> said to him.

So Humphries' mother was a snob, and his father a builder, who was, as he told then *Meanjin* editor Jim Davidson

> the creator of a number of substantial Melbourne
> houses, in jazz moderne with manganese bricks,
> or Spanish Mission with the barley-sugar columns
> and the little grilled windows. I was interested in

houses. I still am interested in the places in which people live, the shells that they inhabit. No-one thought of them as even funny, or thought that life in the suburbs could be funny.

Humphries — and his enduring and increasingly glamorous creation Edna Everage of Moonee Ponds (he didn't want to offend his mother by making Edna from Camberwell) — went on to be one of the most successful cross-dressers and comedians in the world. He was the inspiration for the working-class boy from Balaclava, Graham Kennedy, who was in turn an inspiration for the working-class boy from Reservoir, Graeme Blundell (later Kennedy's biographer). Blundell's dad, Jack, made Kennedy's boots. Blundell wrote: 'Barry transformed not only the comedy business, but also the way we look at ourselves; he was the bridge that took us from the cosy non-threatening world of vaudeville into a dangerous new territory of satire'.

Barry Humphries might be world famous, but Graham Kennedy was Melbourne's first celebrity. 'The whole celebrity thing frightened me', Kennedy said in a 1961 interview with *The Age*'s Graham Perkin (who went on to edit that paper from 1966 to 1975). 'It scared me right through the late 1950s and well into the 1960s. I became a recluse without really wanting to, frightened to move out of my house in Frankston because there were always people by the gates …' Kennedy's style was also distinctively modern, dare I say postmodern, as this interview given to the *Australian* in 1978 suggests:

> I had no particular talent to fall back on. If I made a mistake, there was no alternative to admitting it. If I was uncomfortable, I couldn't help showing it. If I thought the show was bad, I said so, because there was little I could do to improve it.

Melbourne's old-time performers, such as Bob Dyer, had trained in theatre and radio, but television was something else altogether. Kennedy – who'd started, at eighteen, sweeping the floors of radio station 3UZ – stepped into the breach. From May 1957 to December 1969, he was in the studio fronting *In Melbourne Tonight* with his deadpan wit, every now and then breaking into a smile so knowing it was obscene. You can still find some of his in-studio ads on YouTube, and they now seem the quintessential of camp. Kennedy's sidekick, Bert Newton, joined him in 1959 and is still a regular on our television screens.

Sydney didn't really 'get' Graham Kennedy until his game show *Blankety Blanks* in the late 1970s. Indeed the difference in the reception of *IMT* in Melbourne and Sydney set in train the belief that the two cities had totally different senses of humour and required separate programming. Perhaps Sydney's bemusement was one of the reasons Kennedy moved there despite his love of Melbourne – there weren't so many people waiting by the gates. But move or no, Kennedy was called Mr Melbourne for a reason, as Garrie Hutchinson conveys in this article on Kennedy's work:

> From pounds, shillings and pence, Menzies, the dawn of rock'n'roll, short back'n'sides, past decimal currency, the Beatles, long hair, Jean Shrimpton to the dawn of Gough Whitlam … Like footballer Ron Barrasi, Kennedy inspired something that was larger than a cult following around himself. There was something about Melbourne in the late 1950s which created for itself a pantheon of larrikins – Kennedy, Barassi, Sir Henry Bolte, the first heroes of the television age.

Henry Bolte was Victoria's premier from 1955 to 1972 and an arch conservative. It's hard to imagine a leader less likely to lead a state into the swinging sixties and seventies. In fact, you'd have to say things were more swilling than swinging. Look at *The Bar*, the 1954 painting by Melbourne artist John Brack (it hangs in the National Gallery of Victoria), to get a sense of the dehumanising effect of six o'clock closing, which led, inevitably, to the 'six o'clock swill', a ritual in which men downed as much beer as they could before vomiting and/or being ejected onto the street.

Six o'clock closing only ended in Victoria in 1966. This was around the time women won the right to continue working in the public service after marriage and Aboriginal Australians received full citizenship. Censorship was the order of the day, and Victoria's laws were more draconian than those of other states at the time: *Lady Chatterley's Lover*, for example, could be read in South Australia (where Labor's Don Dunstan was premier) but not in Victoria. According to Hilary McPhee, who worked at Penguin Books in 1970, 'over ninety titles remained on the banned list, including many works of literature such as Nabokov's *Lolita*, Hubert Selby Jnr's *Last Exit to Brooklyn*, Henry Miller's *The Tropic of Cancer*, William S. Burroughs' *Naked Lunch*'. No one was reading, let alone producing, plays by Australian writers, and an Australian feature film hadn't had a commercial release since Charles Chauvel's *Jedda* in 1955 – though in 1969 Tim Burstall would change that with *2000 Weeks*.

Tim was married to Betty Burstall, who'd returned from New York in 1967 wanting to re-create 'the vibrancy and immediacy of the small theatres there'. And so a grotty little two-storey shed in a bluestone lane off Grattan Street in Carlton came to transform Australia's cultural life – a particularly remarkable achievement given the era. A group of actors began to rehearse there, but the small and eccentric space quickly defeated them and they moved around the corner into what had once been a pram factory. They called themselves the Australian Performance Group (APG), though they were known colloquially as the Pram Factory. The collective lasted for thirteen years despite famous and ongoing clashes of personality – both central and fringe – over the years. Members included Graeme Blundell, Kerry Dwyer, Jack Hibberd, Bruce Spence (star of the 1971 film *Stork*), Helen Garner, Bill Garner, Bill and Lorna Hannan, playwright David Williamson, satirist Max Gillies, Jon and Ponch Hawkes (later co-founders of Circus Oz), agent and producer John Timlin, John Pinder, Dennis Altman, Martin Armiger, John

Bryson (author of *Evil Angels*), Greig Pickhaver (half of Roy and HG), Mic Conway (the Captain Matchbox Whoopee Band), Jane Clifton, architect Peter Corrigan, Lynette Curran, Barry Dickens, Brian Davies (a local underground filmmaker), Evelyn Krape, Red Symons and playwright John Romeril.

The Pram Factory ran as a collective, and their minutes from 1972 make for slightly alarming reading. Here, for example, is a discussion regarding children:

> Creche: most important a service for APG and possibly audience. Jack Hibberd to investigate. An idea that needs some more discussion, a policy of birth control for the APG, Max Gillies suggested compulsory contraception. This is not expected to go over too well at the next meeting of the Collective.

I was eight years old by then, too old for a creche. Old enough, in fact, to be sent out by my parents to distribute Labor Party brochures, wearing my orange 'It's Time' T-shirt, in the unlikely political hot spot of Toorak Village.

As for this discussion in 1974 about the potentially compromising nature of government funding

… well, editors of most literary journals have such discussions every other day:

> Discussion of the grant received and application
> to Arts Council. A lot of soul searching about
> grants from Liberals or Labors. Lindzee: we're
> really into a capitalist growth thing that we could
> abandon… Cummins: we can't practice politics
> out there and not compromise what we do in
> theatre. Michael Price: if the Libs got into power
> you'd still take money from them.

Politics were changing, and so were eating habits. Blundell ate at Lygon Street's Albion Hotel and he recalls that 'Tony Bilson, a tall young chef as innovative as any playwright … was cooking pot-au-feu of veal shanks, noisettes of pork with apricots and Dijon mustard, and doing shameless things with duck and peaches'. As Michael Harden put it in an essay for *Meanjin*, 'a new generation of chefs and restaurateurs – Stephanie Alexander, Mietta O'Donnell and Gilbert Lau among them – were opening up new businesses, trying to push some boundaries and becoming increasingly frustrated with the legal ties that made it almost impossible for them to get a licence to serve alcohol'. O'Donnell opened Mietta's, her first restaurant, in

North Fitzroy in 1974. Peter Wilmoth described that time in an article he wrote on O'Donnell and Knox after O'Donnell's untimely death in 2001:

> Carlton and Fitzroy types jostled with the curious from Hawthorn and Armadale for a table at Mietta's every night. Knox and O'Donnell juggled front-of-house. In the kitchen in the early days, a former librarian called Stephanie Alexander cooked. Later, a young man of Lebanese background called Greg Malouf came on board. Later still, the restaurant attracted a fellow called Jacques Reymond.

In *Meanjin*, Harden recalled drinking habits were changing: people were beginning to drink less beer and more wine in what could be seen, in part, as reflecting the influence Italian and Greek migrants were beginning to have on the culture. In fact 160 chefs from around the world came to Melbourne during the Olympic Games – Giorgio Angele, whose family owns Brunetti's, arrived in Australia in 1956 as a pastry chef for the Italian Olympic team – and many of them stayed. Over time this had a dramatic impact on Melbourne's food scene.

Ironically, as Melburnians' sense of themselves became more complex, the ocker was being born:

Tim Burstall's film *Stork* (based on a David Williamson play) was released in 1971, starring that 'streaming streak of Pelican shit' Bruce Spence. *The Adventures of Barry McKenzie*, starring Barry Crocker and Barry Humphries, came out in 1972. Both films explored the idea of an Australian character and voice, and they were popular successes despite critical caning. These same critics were more horrified still by *Alvin Purple* (1973), a film that grossed $4 million at the box office at a time when movie tickets cost $2.50. Blundell, one of the key organisers of the Pram Factory, and the film's mostly naked star, earnt $3500 for his performance. He also took with him a curious combination of shame and pride at having made a film that, though challenging Australia's censorship laws, was hated by the burgeoning women's movement – a movement to which his then wife, Kerry Dwyer, belonged.

Challenging the prudery and censorship laws of establishment Melbourne was radical. According to Blundell, 'Some producers really believed that, as artists, we had a mission to rescue citizens from their individual islands of sexual guilt by floating them on a sea of permissiveness'. But feminists weren't so convinced by the idea that nakedness equalled freedom when women (naked or clothed) did not have access to equal pay or working conditions or myriad other legislative and personal rights. This tension – between superficial 'freedoms' and structural change – could be felt everywhere in leftist politics. When Melbourne's first adult bookstore, the Love Art Boutique, opened in 1972 in Victoria Street, West Melbourne, Catholic priests and Nazis sympathisers protested alongside each other, only to be joined soon after by feminists.

This was the context in which women in the APG workshopped a play called 'Betty Can Jump', which they went on to produce and perform. One of the writers of the play was Helen Garner. Claire Dobbin, a member of the collective, describes women's theatre at that time:

> Performing didactic political theatre in the streets is very confrontational and often people were terrorised by us. I can remember an incident when we did a piece of women's theatre outside Coles in Kew, and the shoppers completely panicked. The manager came out and closed the door, locking them inside to protect them from us. The women locked inside went mad and were pounding on the doors. People were really scared; they thought they were witnessing the breakdown of Western civilisation!

Not long after the release of *Alvin Purple*, Blundell was thrown out of the APG because he'd missed a couple of meetings. David Williamson wasn't far behind. Both moved to Sydney, which was no doubt a huge relief to them. As a kid I loved *Alvin Purple*, though my memory is hazy on how I managed to see an R-rated film. Watching it recently I saw what I enjoyed back then: Blundell's slapstick demonstrates the physical style of performance that the APG was known for. They had, as a group, developed a theatrical vocabulary, one that Blundell called 'quasi-naturalistic with absurdist overtones'. You can see this approach in much of the work that emerged from those who spent time at the Pram Factory – in David Williamson's *Don's Party*, in Jack Hibberd's *Dimboola*, in the Captain Matchbox Whoopee Band and in the work of Circus Oz's early performers.

Carlton was – still is – a suburb fed by the University of Melbourne. The advent of Monash (founded in the eastern suburbs in 1958) and Latrobe (founded in the northern ones in 1964) universities coincided with the expansion of higher education. They had no institutional traditions to hold them back and they embraced the radicalism of their times. The Monash Labor Club campaigned against conscription and raised funds for South Vietnam's National Liberation Front. Many of the university's politically active students, such as Michael Hyde, were under ASIO surveillance. It's also been argued that it was Monash students, like John Romeril, who radicalised the APG. By the eighties the situation had flipped: Melbourne Uni became more radical because its wealthier students didn't have to spend all their time working and thus had more time for activism.

I arrived at Monash University in 1980, not knowing the situation had shifted. Radicalism was on the way out, though I am retrospectively amused by the fact that the star of the Monash Labor Club was future Liberal deputy leader Peter Costello. To be honest, though, I hadn't chosen Monash because of its politics, I'd chosen it to escape what I perceived to be Melbourne Uni's smugness.

While my generation were the beneficiaries of much generosity, friendship and professional support from what some dismissively call the Carlton Push, the dynamism of that older generation did create problems for those that followed. We became exhausted by its — and the media's — nostalgia for itself and the lack of understanding that changing times had serious implications for the younger generation's capacity to respond to the world as their parents' generation had. As well, there was the simple fact that the scene was so small there wasn't much space to win over the hearts of the audiences, or the purses of the funding bodies. A David Williamson play still pulls a larger audience than, say, one by Melbourne playwright Tom Wright. And while Wright may not have been talking about Williamson specifically, his comment (made back in 2003) that he was 'so bored with well-written plays about issues. If I see another couch on stage, I'll scream' is one that many younger theatregoers, and practitioners, can relate to. There are solutions to this, of course. In 2004 Alison Croggon wrote:

> The fact that our major theatres are funded so poorly explains why Williamson is a fixture on our subsidised stages. The MTC [Melbourne Theatre Company] receives only 15 per cent of its funding from government sources, which leaves 85 per cent of its budget to be raised by box office and sponsorship. In 1996, the most recent figures I could find, the comparable flagship companies in France, the National Theatres, received 73 per cent of their funding from the State, 21 per cent through the box office and the remaining six per cent from other sales.

The situation essentially remains the same, but despite these funding issues recent years have seen a resurgence of theatre in Melbourne. The Malthouse Theatre in Southbank has revitalised its programme, and several smaller independents, such as Red Stitch and Back to Back, are making their presence powerfully felt.

You can characterise as generational the frustration with, and criticism of, David Williamson and other members of the APG who continue to take up cultural space. But it is also political, morphing into, as Mark Davis has argued, the beginning of 'the new conservatism'.

These simmering, complicated resentments came to a head in the late eighties. I'd finished uni, and my friend Sarah Mathers was working for Almost Managing, an agency run by John Timlin that managed many of the APG's former members. Timlin was developing and producing *Manning Clark's History of Australia: The Musical*. I attended the opening night on 16 January 1988. Six weeks later I attended the – vastly improved – closing night. The show was based on the bold, mad and deeply unfashionable notion of reproducing the themes of Manning Clark's six-volume *A History of Australia* as a costumed musical extravaganza. (This was well before the success of *Keating! The Musical We Had to Have*.) It was an ambitious project and one that failed, though not as spectacularly as its critics liked to suggest.

As Peter Fitzpatrick wrote in his essay on the musical in *Against the Grain: Brian Fitzpatrick and Manning Clark in Australian History and Politics*:

> *History* was reviewed favourably by Helen Thomson in *The Australian*, Jan McGuiness in the *Bulletin*, Barry Oakley in the *Times on Sunday*, Paul Le Petit in the *Sunday Telegraph*, Michael Barnes in the *Sydney Sun-Herald* and John Larkin in the *Sunday Press*; the last three might fairly be described as raves. Unfortunately for the show, the two that were negative were the two most influential in Melbourne – Leonard Radic in *The Age*, Clark Forbes in the *Sun*.

Forbes called the show, among other things, 'the Left-wing cant that spews over the footlights in the name of history' in yet 'another whinge by the revisionists of the Left'.

Reading responses to the show is not unlike reading reviews of Melbourne itself. So controversial did the ill-fated musical become that the *Herald-Sun* commissioned an exposé by finance writer Terry McCrann on the level of government subsidy in the show. Soon after, *Herald* journalist Ben Hills launched a 'special investigation' that concluded that '[W]hen the curtains closed on the disastrous Manning Clark musical … It took with it more than a lot of other people's money – it marked the end of an era for the Carlton push, Australia's cultural commissars.' He also made mention of the fact that Don Watson, one of the writers of the show, was a speechwriter for the then Victorian premier John Cain.

The implication was that the entire production, and indeed Carlton itself, was a left-wing plot. And the program for *History of Australia* certainly gave right-wingers ammunition. Politicians thanked for inspiration inside its cover included then prime minister Bob Hawke, federal ministers Kim Beazley, Gareth Evans, Mick Young and John Button, federal senator Susan Ryan, Victorian premier John Cain and Victorian Minister for Arts Ian Cathie – all from the Australian Labor Party. As Fitzpatrick noted: 'Surely it set a record for the number of politicians to be photographed for a theatre program'. Around the same time there were – unfounded – reports in Brisbane's *Courier-Mail* that Manning Clark had received an Order of Lenin.

It's true to say that if you were on the outside of what Hills calls the Carlton push, it could seem like a closed shop. Even the show's Sydney-based director, John Bell, intimated as much. As Brian Matthews put it, 'A weary John Bell … thoroughly enjoyed "the Melbourne camaraderie and generosity", its benign tribalism, of which Timlin was a quintessential example, but accurately noted that "[i]ts downside is dogged old-mate loyalty and ideological stubbornness"'.

In retrospect it seem clear that *Manning Clark's History of Australia: The Musical* was one of the first victims in the culture wars. While these wars gathered pace during the 1990s, the opening shots were fired in 1984, four years before the musical opened, when Melbourne historian Geoffrey Blainey gave a speech saying that public opinion would not support the rate of Asian immigration. In 1988 Blainey resigned from the University of Melbourne over the tensions those remarks had triggered between himself and his colleagues.

I was both a beneficiary of those Carlton loyalties and caught up in the generational politics that followed. The way I ended up working in publishing is — or was — a typical Melbourne story. My dad drank at Percy's in Carlton. A lot of writing types went there on a Friday evening, including Don Watson, who was, at the time, in a relationship with Hilary McPhee. Hilary was looking for tenants to rent the terrace house she owned in Cecil Street, Fitzroy. I moved in there, with a group of friends, in 1987. Hilary noticed that I was writing reviews for the arts section of the *Melbourne Times* and offered me some work reading manuscripts.

When I worked for McPhee Gribble they were based in a warehouse in Cecil Street that had once been a sewing factory. The flourishing lavender garden that Diana Gribble planted out the front is still going, but the building now houses a dance studio. When I first started visiting the place to drop off editorial reports, a young woman called Robyn Annear worked there. She would regale me with stories of working on archaeological digs in Little Lonsdale Street and the remnants of the brothels that had been found there. Robyn has since written several historical books about Melbourne, including the fabulous tale of the city's beginnings, *Bearbrass*. Bearbrass was, as Robyn explained, Melbourne's first name, a 'mis-rendering of *Birrarung*, meaning "river of mists" in the language of the Wurundjeri people'. When Robyn knocked back the chance to be a trainee editor at McPhee Gribble — she said she'd rather be a postie — I was offered the position.

I took it for granted that my first serious job would be at a company run by two women, both of whom invested a lot of time in training me, not just to be the best editor I could be but the best person. Twenty years later, however, the radical nature of my first and most formative work environment is clear to me. I often think now about how we worked as a group, the ideas and conversations that we shared, the confidence we were given, and the support we were offered. As Hilary wrote, 'This was how we all expected to work at a time of our lives when the public and private overlapped so much the division had no meaning. But that doesn't start to convey the complex web of relationships that held the place together.' It was a beautiful curse in a way, and while I've worked in conventional office environments since, I've never settled comfortably into them.

Much of the more interesting, but unrepeatable, gossip to be told about McPhee Gribble involves the well-used couch where we sat every morning for cups of coffee served from large enamel pots. In the evenings we often went for a second sitting and had a drink together. When McPhee Gribble was sold to Penguin Books in 1989, I bought that couch and went on to lug it with me from house to house before finally taking it to Sydney. By that time its springs were so bad that its base rested on the floor. The couch didn't make it back to Melbourne, but the bookshelves full of all the books McPhee Gribble published over those years did. They've become something of a touchstone for all the work I've done, or attempted to do, since. McPhee Gribble was the first time I began to understand that the work you did in the world had meaning. Passions could be turned into something that existed outside yourself: they could become books.

After McPhee Gribble lost its independence, Di Gribble went on (with Eric Beecher) to set up Text Publishing and then to buy Steven Mayne's *Crikey*, which is one of the most influential and widely read news websites in the country. Two years after Penguin bought McPhee Gribble, Hilary became a publisher at Pan Macmillan. She later headed up the Australia Council.

When I was appointed publisher of McPhee Gribble/Penguin at the age of twenty-eight, my appointment was referred to as 'window dressing'.

Perhaps in reaction to this, my publishing was most confident when I was working with books about my generation and responding to the politics of the times I lived in, books such as *I Was a Teenage Fascist* by David Greason, which was about the National Front in Melbourne during the 1970s; *Glad All Over: The Countdown Years 1974–1987* by Peter Wilmoth, a book about the ABC pop show *Countdown*; and *Holding the Man* by Timothy Conigrave, the story of two young men who met and fell in love at Xavier College in Melbourne and later fell victim to the AIDS epidemic. I stayed on at McPhee Gribble/ Penguin as publisher for two years before heading to Sydney where I worked as a publisher for Allen & Unwin. It was there that I published Mark Davis's *Gangland: Cultural Elites and the New Generationalism*.

Hilary and I have been friends for almost twenty-five years now, but I didn't know she'd worked at *Meanjin* until I read her book *Other People's Words*. I was struck by how her experience of the place echoed mine, despite the fact that we'd worked there forty years apart. What she had learnt from Clem Christesen, *Meanjin*'s first editor, she had gone on to teach me, all those years ago. She wrote: 'My job ... imprinted on me a sense that editors should be active not passive, that grammar and punctuation and spelling meant much – Christesen was meticulous – but that what was being said meant more'.

During Christesen's 34-year editorial reign, *Meanjin* attracted contributions and debate from the leading figures of Australian letters, as well as providing an Australian audience for leading international writers. It was known primarily as a literary journal but it reflected the breadth of contemporary thinking. In the 1950s Christesen faced the challenge of maintaining the editorial independence of a left-leaning journal – as well as funding and institutional support – in the Cold War climate, even having to appear before the Royal Commission on Espionage. He once said he wanted *Meanjin* to 'make clear the connection between literature and politics', something I tried to emulate during my time at the journal.

Christesen was not an easy man. This letter, written to the equally combative author Kylie Tennant, is not atypical:

> Let's face it my dear, for most of this journal's life you have not been a contributor … So far as I was aware you were not even a subscriber. And during those long years of struggle – and believe me I am not exaggerating – you gave me no help at all.

Christesen was right. Editing a journal is not as much fun as you would hope. Christesen struggled for money more than we do these days, though perhaps was more rewarded by an era that valued public intellectuals — a role that the editor of a journal such as *Meanjin* is inevitably expected to take up. Christesen's enduring mission was to define what it meant to be Australian, and A.A. Phillips' famous essay published in *Meanjin* in 1950, 'The Cultural Cringe', still impacts on conversations today and it's title has entered the lexicon.

But things have changed. *Meanjin* is no longer run by a man 'looking like a Chicago detective out of a noir thriller — puffing his Craven As, pacing the floor, waving his arms around as he emphasised what he was trying to do with the magazine', as Hilary McPhee put it. The journal lost its independence in the months before I came on board in early 2008, becoming an imprint of Melbourne University Publishing. This was an event that, as Simon Hughes wrote in *Crikey*, provoked 'the Melbourne literary scene fracturing along unsuspected tribal lines'. Certainly it was a form of governance that diminished the seniority of the position of editor.

A few weeks after I took up the editorship of

Meanjin in 2008, I went back to the *Meanjin* office at 131 Barry Street, Carlton. The journal had been based there from 1999 but had just moved to Melbourne University Publishing. It was a melancholy visit in some ways – there were files left in piles to be sorted through and letterheads using past logos stacked up around the place waiting for the recycling. The old couch that Christesen used to sleep on was still hidden in a corner, and paintings he'd done were still hanging on the walls.

There was a copy of *Meanjin* from 2004 on the desk too, and in it was a tribute by John McLaren, a former editor of fellow Australian literary journal *Overland*. He'd written:

> If we consider the way successive editors
> have remade *Meanjin* we can see how each has
> contributed a distinctive quality to it. Yet no
> editor is completely free. *Meanjin*'s founding editor
> had to find or make a place for the new journal,
> and the succeeding editors have had to start from
> the place they inherited. Their task has been to
> reimagine that place for new times …

I didn't have Christesen's confidence that *Meanjin* possessed a grand mission: that it could do something as grandiose, perhaps impossible, as define what it is to be Australian. Such clarity of purpose was the privilege of an earlier century, one that could not exist in such a populated and politically fragmented world. Instead I was motivated to capture the myriad ways in which culture is made – at the very time that both the ways in which culture are made and the ways in which we talk about these things appear to be refracting at greater and greater speed. Sometimes the job felt like trying to focus the light cast off a mirror ball.

When I was at *Meanjin* I felt caught, as I had when I became publisher of McPhee Gribble/Penguin, in the insidious position of trying to honour an institution's history while finding a way to give it a future. In both cases it seemed I failed, and certainly if I worked in publishing again I would want to be part of something new, rather than attempt to keep something old alive.

Even though things at work had not yet come to a head, these things were on my mind – they usually are – in April 2009 as I headed to a small production studio off St Kilda Road to film an episode of the SBS quiz show *ADbc*. One of my co-panellists was Graeme Davison, the author of *The Rise and Fall of Marvellous Melbourne*. That book begins with the opening of the International Exhibition at Melbourne's new Royal Exhibition Building, the city's coming of age:

> His Excellency the Marquis of Normanby, and
> a party of visiting dignitaries, emerged from the
> Domain and proceeded down St Kilda Road
> towards the city. Only thirty years before, an
> exuberant publican had driven his coach down
> that same stretch of road blowing a trumpet
> and waving a union jack to announce Victoria's
> separation from New South Wales.

It's possible that Davison, like me, felt his dignity under attack as we tried to answer a series of questions about the First World War and the like while looking good and being uproariously funny. We did our best, but we should have both put our foot down when it came to eating a 'historical dish' that turned out to be based on an ancient Chinese recipe for silkworm omelette. I almost choked, and I wondered how it was that my career had come to this. It was a timely reminder – Melbourne is good at them – not to take myself too seriously. As my friend and current *Overland* editor Jeff Sparrow said to me after watching the episode when it went to air a few months later, 'I bet Clem Christesen never had to eat worms'. Well, yes and no. He did suffer the – necessary – indignity of being pushed out of the editorship of the journal after thirty-three years of service. Or, as Jim Davidson, Christesen's successor, said in his lecture to commemorate *Meanjin*'s seventieth birthday in late 2010, 'Every editorship ends like that: all those arrows in your backside. And, over thirty-three years, Clem had accumulated quite a lot of them.' I managed a mere year to each of Christesen's decades before the arrows got me, just as those birthday celebrations were taking place.

A few days after eating those worms, I went to the opening of *The Independent Type: Books and Writing in Victoria* at the State Library of Victoria. The exhibition was curated by Steve Grimwade (now the director of the Melbourne Writers Festival) and included a range of materials that conveyed what was special about Melbourne's publishing life and the ways stories are told in this town. Objects included a possum-skin storytelling cloak, a charcoal and brown ochre painting by Indigenous leader William Barak, an old edition of *Overland*, a cover of Frank Hardy's *Power Without Glory*, and a photo of Hilary and Diana sitting together on the McPhee Gribble couch. When I saw that photo I stood there for some time. I'm not sure whether it was the suggestion that the historical moment that McPhee Gribble represented had passed, whether it was the fact I was now the age Hilary and Di were when it was taken, or whether it had just been a long day. Whatever the reason, I stood in front of that photo and began to cry.

Winter

Winter descended, and we entered another phase in our annual battle with the Cape Lilac. It dropped its leaves and the courtyard was lined with what was at first a velvety green carpet but soon turned into slushy leaf mush. In Sydney people call Melbourne 'Bleak City', and at this time of year that's an apt description. The city grid funnels cold south-westerly winds up from the sea. It's cold but there's no frost or snow to break up the grey. And though our winters are warmer now, they are still long and unpleasantly clammy, and one is inevitably depressed by the end of them. Our iconic terrace houses are beautiful, with their combination of Victorian English restraint and exuberant New World iron lace frippery, but tend towards damp and cold.

June began with a dash out of Melbourne to visit my mother, who'd been unwell. She was at Alexandra Hospital, and that meant a trip through fire country. While Virginia and I had driven north in the preceding months, we'd gone straight up the Hume Freeway to avoid the worst of the damage – to do otherwise seemed ghoulish. Even then we saw plenty of black earth and signs to towns like Flowerdale, where eight people lost their lives and an estimated 80 per cent of residents became homeless. But the time had come, we'd decided, to take a look for ourselves. We drove along Kinglake's eastern boundary before heading west into the town itself. The gums around Kinglake East flashed new green, vivid against black charcoal, so at first I felt encouraged. But in the township itself people whose lives had been destroyed by heat were now huddled into caravans and pre-fab villages, freezing. West of the town looked as if it had been carpet bombed. Although I had expected devastation, I was shocked. Virginia grew up in Mount Macedon, which had been badly burnt on Ash Wednesday in 1983, so she was more familiar with such ruined landscapes. But despite, or because of, that history, she also found the drive very unsettling.

We drove home a different way a few hours later as the late afternoon light settled in, past the Cathedral Range and Marysville. The weak winter light made the scene even grimmer than it already was. The soil around Narbethong was scorched as Kinglake West had been and there was still no regrowth. There were pitch-black stripes on the Cathedral Range even darker — if that were possible — than the earth on either side of them, as if fireballs had raced up or down a path and scorched it even more thoroughly. The temperatures recorded in these areas had been so great that the fires simmered underground, killing the seeds as well as animals that had retreated there in an attempt to survive. The final part of our trip was along Acheron Way, which is lined by soaring mountain ashes, the tallest trees in Victoria. The area was badly hit in 1939 but this time around had miraculously survived.

That same weekend I went for a walk with a friend, novelist Michelle de Kretser. She was moving to Sydney and it was no accident, I suppose, that she'd chosen winter to leave us. I drove to her house in Richmond to see her. Richmond is a suburb that boasts the greatest number of sky-signs in the state. The most famous of these, the Skipping Girl formerly known as Little Audrey, has been the subject of many a conservation campaign. But you can't let the Skipping Girl's charms blind you to sights like the 31-metre Slade Knitwear neon (which is, according to Melbourne designer Stephen Banham, 'one of the most sublimely beautiful signs in Melbourne') or the Pelaco Shirt Factory sign (erected during a dubious advertising campaign that featured an Aboriginal man wearing nothing but a Pelaco shirt, saying, 'Mine tinkit dey fit'). The Pelaco sign was inspiration for the Pelaco Brothers, a band featuring Stephen Cummings, Joe Camilleri and Peter Lillie among others. It also got a guernsey in Richard Lowenstein's iconic 1986 film *Dogs in Space*, which charted Melbourne's inner-city music scene of the late seventies.

I had always associated the Pelaco sign with my friend Sarah Mathers' father, who lived in a tiny house beneath it for 25 years before his death in 2004. In many ways, Peter Mathers was an archetypal Melbourne figure. In 1967 he won the Miles Franklin Literary Award for his novel *Trap*, and when Sarah and I lived together we'd go and see his plays at the Carlton Courthouse Theatre. But despite his distinction as a writer who pushed language into a range of outrageous, punning shapes, Peter lives on in my memory most of all as an extraordinary gardener. I always envied those who received remainders of his novel *The Wort Papers*. He had composted the unsold copies but dug them up on special occasions to give as gifts. The rotting books, full of soil and chewed through by worms, seemed both symbolic and practical.

Michelle lived off Swan Street, which is the home of Dimmeys. Melbourne's oldest department store was built in 1853, and the enormous ornamental clock above it is a particular favourite in our family: on my first trip overseas my brother sent me a letter in which he told me that the giant ball above the clock had fallen off Dimmeys and rolled down Swan Street towards the MCG, killing several people along the way. I believed him. The clock can be admired for its use of type as numerals – it's one of the few places in the world where the time can be 'an E past a D'. As I write this, plans are under review for an eleven-storey tower to be built on the site. While the clock tower has a heritage listing, there is the danger that it will simply be entombed like Melbourne's Coops (Melbourne Central) Shot Tower. That tower was built in 1890 and saved from demolition in 1973, only to be whacked under an 84 metre-high conical glass roof with an R.M. Williams shop in its base. Some days it seems to me that the fly in amber approach to conserving a city is worse than no policy at all, but the real issue is lazy design solutions to complex cultural problems.

It's hard to park in Richmond's smaller streets without hitting the cars on the other side of the road when you reverse in. After I finally found a spot in Michelle's narrow one-way street, I knocked on the door and was pounced upon by dogs. We drank tea from her eclectic little teacups before we headed down to the Yarra River.

Michelle, her bouncy big black dog Ollie and I walked down past a power station, along the river towards Hawthorn. We walked through Loys Paddock, which had once been kept by the soft-drink company as a place to graze its horses when they weren't pulling carts. Some of the European trees originally planted in the paddock survive, but many of them have died and the river gums are beginning to reassert themselves. This pattern is recurring all over Melbourne, as gums are planted in the place of dying European trees. We walked along the track where the Yarra once ran before it was diverted to make way for what is now known as the Monash Freeway. The river has lost several of its more meandering loops over the 175 years of white settlement: it's straighter, wider and an entire 3 kilometres shorter than it was when Europeans first arrived.

The path Michelle, Ollie and I were walking, along the Yarra through Richmond, Hawthorn and Kew towards Dights Falls, is a favourite walk or bike ride for people who live in this area. It cuts through ancient landscapes. As Yarra biographer Kristin Otto wrote, 'The sandstone, siltstone, mudstone strata that reveal themselves by Dights Falls, among other places, are four-hundred-million-year-old seabed that's folded, faulted and eroded'. The river outlined, in part, the territory of the Wurundjeri people. In 1835 on the banks of one of the Yarra's tributaries, the Merri Creek, eight elders supposedly signed the papers that 'gave' John Batman the 'right' to Melbourne.

It is symptomatic of Melbourne's attitude towards the Yarra that shifting a waterway that had been cutting its way through volcanic rock for over 300 million years was seen as more straightforward than diverting an as-yet-unbuilt freeway. Several powerful eruptions, the most recent 800 000 years ago, had failed to destroy the river – they'd simply forced it to embed its course all over again. Something of the stubbornness and recalcitrance of the river's spirit is captured in a Wurundjeri version of its creation, in which its beds are formed by the heels of a young boy who is being dragged along the ground by an angry old man. After white settlement the river kept fighting, and there were notable floods in Melbourne in 1839, 1848, 1863, 1891, 1934, 1972 and 1989. Elizabeth Street, the lowest point of the CBD, is still particularly susceptible to flooding. In its early years water coursed through it at such speed that humans and horses were drowned. In 1972 flood waters rose to the heights of the awnings of buildings. Water always finds its level, it seems. This regular flooding was a direct result of the profound lack of understanding about how water moved through the land before it was developed.

Once Michelle left, it wasn't long before she was calling me from her new house in Dulwich Hill and talking about Sydney's weather with all the passion of a woman falling in love. I felt as if she were dating an ex of mine and wanted to protest that under all those good looks Sydney didn't have much going on. In truth, I was jealous. Not only was I going to miss Michelle, I was confronted by her choice, the reverse of the one I'd made when I returned from Sydney in 2001. It seemed that having written a love letter to Melbourne in the form of her 2007 novel *The Lost Dog*, she had freed herself from the place – she certainly sounded like a woman who had no intention of coming back. I understood why she wouldn't. There is a physicality to life in Sydney that is intensely seductive and rewarding. St Kilda, south of the city, has never competed with Sydney's beaches, despite, as Paul Kelly's song goes, 'its one sweet promenade'.

St Kilda's Esplanade is worth singing about, there's no doubt about that. The palm-lined boulevard hugs the wide sweep of Port Phillip Bay, a bay so shallow and flat that on silky dark-grey days it can be hard to tell where the land ends and the sea begins. You can wade out a hundred metres alongside St Kilda Pier, or at Elwood a little further south, and still be just past your knees. The bay is a bit of a newcomer, geologically speaking, and was formed about 10 000 years ago at the end of the last ice age. The sea level rose to drown what were then the lower reaches of the Yarra River's plains, wetlands and lakes. The Yarra and other tributaries flowed down what is now the middle of the bay, forming a lake in its southern reaches.

The Wurundjeri believe the bay was created when Bunjil, the creator spirit, was walking across open hunting lands with two boys. He told them that they could open the magical containers full of water back at their campground. When they did, there was a deluge. The boys ran this way and that in search of dry land but could not find any. Bunjil took pity on them, tossing a rock ahead of the advancing waters and ordering the waters to stop rising. That massive rock can still be seen on the shoreline near Brighton. This image of a rising sea continued post-settlement. In 1987 Melbourne-based science fiction writer George Turner wrote a novel called *The Sea and Summer* that imagines Melbourne in the middle of the 21st century. A young boy is taken to 'see' the ocean for his birthday, though what he's shown is a concrete wall that stretches to the horizon. The boy's mother explains, 'This is Elwood and there was a beach here once. I used to paddle here. Then the water came up and there were the storm years and the pollution and the water became too filthy.'

That's a possible future, but the Port Phillip Bay of today is about light. Cloudy days transform the bay into a steel-grey expanse that glints and flashes in the sunlight. The bay acts as a mirror, reflecting back the edges of the city and the sky above. It's that quality of light, as well as the sea breeze, that draws people to it.

In the middle of the 1800s, St Kilda was developed as one of Melbourne's wealthier suburbs for 'colonists of a better sort' – the sort who could afford to live a short carriage ride away from the centre of town and avail themselves of the sea air. Its pier – still a favoured place for a Sunday afternoon walk – was built in 1853, and a kiosk was built at the end of it in 1904. That kiosk burnt down in 2003 and provoked a dilemma that perhaps sums up Melbourne's prevarication around issues of identity: should an identical kiosk be built or a structure that suggested Melbourne's more modern spirit? Disappointingly, the council went for the carbon copy.

The suburb's very beautiful botanical gardens were developed as early as 1859 but St Kilda is not a Victorian suburb. The opening of Luna Park amusement park in 1912 gave the place a hint of New York's Coney Island, and most of its development took place after the First World War. Its era is predominantly Art Deco. Perhaps because of this aesthetic, and the palm trees that line the Esplanade, St Kilda evokes the world of film – and cities, like Los Angeles, where films are made. As if in response to this, it's where many of Melbourne's filmmakers are based today.

Many of the buildings that make St Kilda so distinctive were built in the 1920s, including cinemas such as the Palais (with an interior designed by Walter Burley Griffin) and the Victory (now known as the National Theatre). Author Brian Matthews grew up in St Kilda and describes 'going to the Palais Pictures on a Friday night' as 'a matter of stately and unswerving ritual', before describing the source of the pleasure to be found there: 'Once ensconced, the old man would light up the first of his six going-to-the-pictures cigarettes. The next would be during the newsreel and 'shorts'; then one at interval, two during the main feature and one walking home.'

In the 1930s and 1940s, the influx of Europeans fleeing anti-Semitism meant St Kilda became the centre of Melbourne's Jewish community. Acland Street became famous for its Jewish cafes and cake shops, and one of these cafes was immortalised by Arnold Zable in his third book, 2001's *Cafe Scheherazade*:

> In Acland Street, St Kilda, there stands a cafe
> called Scheherazade. As to how it came to have
> such a name, therein lies a story. Many stories in
> fact, recounted at a table in the back room where
> the proprietors, Mr and Mrs Zeleznikow, Avram

and Masha, sit most nights of the week and eat, hold court, greet customers, check accounts, argue and reminisce. What else is there to do on this rain-sodden Melbourne night, as pedestrians rugged in overcoats stroll on pavements glistening grey, past shops laden with slices of Black Forest cake where they pause and hesitate, before succumbing to the temptation to buy, well, just one slice. Perhaps two.

The suburb is visually dominated by the greedy gaping clown mouth of Luna Park's entrance at the lower end of the Esplanade. That creepy fairground feel has, at times, infected St Kilda, and it's suffered from being the suburb people go to have *fun* in: fun including things like smoking in the cinema, hearing live music at the awesomely beautiful but grotty Esplanade Hotel, paying for sex and buying drugs. This slide from decadence into something harder and tougher took place after the Second World War. Prostitution moved from the centre of Melbourne to the beach, drug culture began to flourish, and all those genteel mansions were turned into seedy boarding houses. By the 1960s St Kilda's fall from grace meant it was affordable for artists and musicians – a phase typified by Tolarno, a hotel, cafe and gallery owned by bohemian art world figures Georges and Mirka Mora. In recent years Tolarno, like much of St Kilda, has been sold, renovated and gentrified, though the famous murals Mirka painted when she ran the place are still intact.

These days there is a curious tension between newcomers and longer-term residents of the suburb, a tension most obviously played out in the battle over street prostitution. People are attracted to the area's boho feel but don't want to be mistaken for prostitutes by cruising tourists. Nor do they like living with the poverty and violence that goes with the drug scene. Media commentator Leslie Cannold found herself stuck in the middle of this ethical dilemma in 2002 when the local council attempted to solve the street prostitution problem:

> What they decided to do was to try to herd
> the problem into containment areas that would
> contain sex worker centres where clients could be
> serviced. One of the sites they chose for this role
> was a busy main street bordered by a number of
> quiet solely residential streets, including mine ...
> Their thinking was based on a major report by
> the Attorney General Street Prostitution Advisory
> Group ... but it soon became abundantly clear
> that idealised containment zones representing the

values and needs of all stakeholders simply didn't exist in the reality of St Kilda.

The situation remains unresolved.

As a kid, of course, I found the tension that characterises the suburb pretty exciting. In fact, the first time I ever caught the tram was the 69 to the National Theatre on the corner of Carlisle and Barkly streets, where I started, and ended, my brief career in the theatre (I got as far as learning how to *be* a tree). Budding talent aside, a weekend trip to the beach or Luna Park — where I would, without fail, freak out as I got to the entrance — followed by Leo's Spaghetti Bar on Fitzroy Street and then cakes in Acland Street was as good as it got.

Leo's was opened to coincide with the 1956 Olympic Games, when it was, as hoped, frequented by many of the Games' participants. Since then the facade has changed several times. What began as three narrow shopfronts was demolished at the beginning of the seventies to make up the current eccentric facade, which is actually, as designer Stephen Banham pointed out, 'made up of typography spelling out its name'. If you eat your spaghetti at the front bench, you're eating off the middle stroke of the letter E. When Banham called Leo's owners, they were bemused that tourists now come and look at this architectural quirk: 'At a rough guess (because nobody can remember exactly) they estimated that the first shop would have been where the letter L is, the second the E and the third the O'.

Despite St Kilda's charms, Melbourne is not a city you're going to understand if you orient yourself towards the bay. You're closer to the life of this land if you stand on St Kilda Pier with your back to the water and look a kilometre or so north-east, across to Albert Park Lake and the parklands that surround it. Internationally, and somewhat controversially, it's become known as the site of Melbourne's Grand Prix, but for locals it's a perfect 5 kilometres around and a favourite place for weekend walks — despite the fact that some months it's so shallow it's barely 6 inches deep and the marshlands spotted through it are dry. Dozens of water birds gather here, the most magnificent being the native black swan. When their necks are extended they're as tall as a human, and they have a wingspan of up to 2 metres. When they unfold those awesome wings — as they often do, with a flourish that suggests it's mainly for show — you see their snow-white flight feathers contrasting their coal black bodies. If you walk the lake in early spring when their fluffy grey cygnets have hatched, you wouldn't want to take one on in a fight. When the water is shallow those necks are longer than needed to feed, bottoms up and necks down, on the lake floor; though after rains they need every inch of their advantage.

When I met Gary Presland, author of *First People*, he said to me, 'If you like an area you call it a wetland. If you don't like it you call it a swamp.' It's fitting, then, that this sometimes beautiful, strangely shallow lake is a remnant of the South Swamp, an enormous salt lagoon that formed a part of the delta where the Yarra met the sea. As a consequence it kept on flooding the entire area now known as South Melbourne and St Kilda until it was sealed up in the late 1880s and from 1890 filled with freshwater drained from the Yarra. Elwood's canals were also built around this time in an attempt to solve the same problem.

So, to make sense of Melbourne, look to its erratic, brackish wetlands; its muddy, beautiful rivers; its sometimes smelly old lagoons and lakes; and the sudden shock of those moments after heavy rain when the city's cup briefly runneth over. Acclaimed author J.M. Coetzee once wrote:

As I watch the trickle that runs through the park turn into a torrent, the deeply alien nature of floodwater is brought home to me. The flood is not puzzled or disconcerted by obstacles or barriers it finds in its way. Puzzlement, disconcertment are not in its repertoire. Barriers are simply overrun, obstacles shoved aside. The nature of water, as the pre-Socratics might have said, is to flow. For water to be puzzled, to hesitate, even for an instant, would be against nature.

Replace the word 'water' with 'fire' and the sentiment holds true. Both these elements now loom large in modern Melbourne's consciousness. Not enough of the first, too much of the second.

Statistics released by the Bureau of Meteorology at the end of July 2009 indicated that Melbourne was now Australia's driest city. With just 158 millimetres falling since 1 January that year, Melbourne was almost twice as dry as Adelaide and Sydney. If our water storages fell to 20.3 per cent, as they were threatening to do, the city would be hit with stage 4 restrictions, prohibiting all watering of gardens and sporting grounds. In a matter of ten years or so, jokes about how much it rains in Melbourne have become quaintly archaic. Those number plates declaring us the Garden State are even more arcane.

After a particularly dry spell of a couple of years, one which broke in 2007, I remember waking at dawn with my heart racing and a great air of expectation. A few moments later a gentle rain began and it was the loveliest, the most fragile of sounds.

The latest information from the CSIRO identifies the following trends for the south-east of Australia: increased average summer temperatures and more extreme events. That means more hot days and more months on end with no rain at all, but it also means increased rainfall during storms. The damage caused by the current drought would not be healed by a few months of heavy rain (and in 2010 there would be a good deal of it); it would take several years of above average rainfall. That is the difference between weather and climate: short-term ebbs and flows versus long-term trends. Since 1950 the average temperature in Melbourne has already risen a degree. At a conservative estimate the greater Melbourne area could experience average annual temperature increases of another 0.5 degrees Celsius by 2020 and 1.4 degrees by 2050. Rise in temperature will be accompanied by a drop in average annual rainfall and a consequent reduction of water flowing into Melbourne's main reservoirs of 7 per cent by 2020 and 18 per cent by 2050. At the same time, Melbourne's projected population expansion is 1 million people over the next twenty years. After 150 years of battling water in Melbourne, Bunjil's containers have run dry. Puzzled, disconcerted, water is hesitating. We are in danger of running out.

In June, Melbourne's drawn-out gangland wars took another twist. Judy Moran, a crime matriarch who had already lost her sons and husband in the bloodshed, was arrested for (and later found guilty of) the murder of her brother-in-law, Des, in a cafe in Union Road, Ascot Vale. His last words were reported as being, unsurprisingly, 'Oh shit'. While relatively regular gangland killings had taken place in Carlton and Brunswick, and it was perfectly possible to walk those suburbs and point at various pubs and restaurants saying, 'Wasn't so and so killed here?' I, suburbia-phobe that I am, feel much more nervous walking the leafy suburb of Hawthorn, where I grew up.

People feed their antipathies however they can, which is perhaps why the manner of Eloise Worledge's taking from deep in the heart of

Melbourne middle-class suburbia — from a bed-room, from a family, from a house in bayside Beaumaris — made such an impression when it occurred in the summer of 1976. The stories of the grief that descended upon the Worledges in the months and years after Eloise's abduction made their mark also. Her parents, Patsy and Lindsay, were effectively separated, though living under the one roof. The disarray in their personal lives led to the unfounded suspicion that they were involved in their daughter's death. In effect, the charade of their marriage, the faux perfection of their home, was seen to be a crime in itself.

Similar stories were spun after thirteen-year-old Karmein Chan was taken at knifepoint from her wealthy family's Templestowe home in 1991. Her body was found a year later at a creek in Thom-astown. Karmein's parents worked long hours in their restaurant and Karmein was looking after her sisters when she was taken. In the media coverage that followed, much was made of this notion of latchkey parenting. The suburbs are spaces where perfection is possible, the argument seems to be. It's just everyone who lives in them who fails. This smug sense of certainty combined with the inev-itability of failure are what one rebels against, a rebellion that has fuelled many great Melbourne comedians. Although you could argue, of course, that the anxiety provoked by suburbia creates a snobbery that's as ridiculous in its way as Louisa Humphries' fear of bought cakes.

Television also fed into my perceptions. In the early seventies I was old enough to want to watch the Sydney-based *Number 96,* though my parents said I was too young. I remember hiding behind the couch one evening and watching it over their shoulders (though it now occurs to me that they must have known I was there). There was something very appealing to me about the idea of a group of people in an apartment block that was a world entire to itself. Certainly the notion of a group of people – a group that included Italians and homosexuals and an impossibly large-breasted blonde called Bev who was played by an impossibly large-breasted actress known only as Abigail – all living at close quarters in Paddington was far more exciting than what I understood of the suburbs as represented by *Neighbours* a decade later. That show, which began in 1985, is one of Australia's most successful television series. It's set in the fictional Ramsay Street, Erinsborough, but is filmed in Melbourne's Pin Oak Court, Vermont South. The two shows say something, albeit accidentally, about the tensions between the cosmopolitan and built-up inner city (represented for me when I was young by Sydney) and the seemingly endless suburbs of Melbourne. But there is no doubt that the outer suburbs, in particular, have iconic power: George Miller's 1979 film *Mad Max* was filmed in Lara, a flat anonymous township west of Melbourne towards Geelong, not far from the sewage farm at Werribee. In that film's amplified vision of the dangerous anonymity of that featureless place – neither city nor country – lie some of the most memorable and loaded images of Melbourne ever committed to screen.

In early 2009, Sydney director David Michôd was in Melbourne shooting his debut feature *Animal Kingdom*, a film that went on to considerable critical and box office success in 2010. The leafy middle-class suburb of Ivanhoe is home to Australia's oldest book group, one which has been meeting since the 1920s, and certainly isn't an obvious spot to make a film about gangland killing. But Michôd capitalised on the strange tension between aspiration and reality that characterises some suburbs. He was also keen to avoid trams, and as Ivanhoe is more than 10 kilometres out of Melbourne, the tracks never made it out there. As he explained:

> I very specifically didn't want to put Melbourne
> landmarks in the back of shots. I wanted to steer
> away from that impression of Melbourne that
> I have based on a number of movies that have
> been set there. The impression that people get
> based on the movies is very often one of a cutesy,
> quaint village of trams and Victorian frills. My
> experience of the city is that it's a much bigger,
> badder city.

Hawthorn's clay-ridden soils challenged my parents when they were setting up our then (and, thanks to climate change, again) trendy native garden. That clay provided the developing suburb with a crucial industry: Melbourne's early brickmakers tapped its soil, leaving the area scattered with pits and quarries. It was to one of those quarries — long abandoned — that my high school mates and I went to smoke at lunchtime, returning to school reeking of the fennel that flourished there.

Many of Hawthorn's first settlers were German immigrants. One of these families, the Holzers, became brickmakers, and in 1888 they offered pits that were now wastelands to the council. These became the Central Gardens. Eventually eight Holzer claypits were joined to become parklands, and below them the council built a network of drains that are known these days as the Maze. One sunny winter morning in June, Jeff Sparrow and I headed to Hawthorn to meet up with a co-founder of the Cave Clan so he could take us down.

One of the Cave Clan's founders, Wes, is, in fact, a great-great-great-grandson of Martin Holzer, but this morning we were meeting with his colleague Dougo. The organisation they helped found is 23 years old and has chapters in every state and affiliates the world over. Its success is testimony to the power of secret places.

I had been unaccountably nervous about the excursion — and it wasn't only the thought of walking underground for several hours that was making me claustrophobic. It was returning to the suburb where I'd lived for most of my childhood. Anxiety gripped me when we pulled up at the car park of Glenferrie Road Shopping Centre and tried to locate our meeting place. Predictably we'd driven to the wrong shopping centre so we had to walk along Burwood Road for a kilometre or so (almost, as it turned out, directly above the drain we were to walk through an hour later). I started muttering darkly about the bland horrors of Hawthorn, which led Jeff to brood on what he felt were the even blander horrors of Brighton, the pretty beachside suburb where he'd grown up. Frankly, getting to the potential danger of the drain itself was going to be a relief.

The memories that besieged me were of adolescence and its awkwardness: trying to carry several chocolate mousse set in long-stemmed champagne glasses when I waitressed in a French restaurant tucked into the arcade under the train line, drinking Brandivino from a paper bag at a footy oval on a wintry night with a group of friends and then feeling horrendously ill, riding my bike down a particular street because I had a crush on a boy who lived there, a tennis lesson behind the library with a coach who told me girls were no good at tennis and thus encouraged me to quit at the end of my first and only class.

I made myself remember the good things, like the popularity-garnering Clark Rubber pool in the backyard. If it was over 30 degrees for a couple of days in a row, we declared it a heatwave. Winters were often so cold that we'd wake up to ice on the windscreen of the car – a sight I haven't seen in inner-city Melbourne for several decades. It rained. A lot. We played backyard cricket with neighbours and had Monopoly marathons. There was the rogue great-uncle who attempted to lure my brother to barrack for Hawthorn by plying him with the team's jumpers and scarves. It's possible too that my brother was tempted by that now famous graffiti, sprayed onto a sign outside a local church not far from where we lived. 'What would you do if Christ came to Hawthorn?' the sign asked. 'Move Peter Hudson to Centre-Half Forward' was the definitive answer.

When daylight saving was trialled in 1971 those first long evenings seemed wondrous: roller-skating down Auburn Road to the local shops until after eight at night. The settling in of a lush blue twilight that lasts until after nine through December and January remains one of the things I love most about Melbourne, though I didn't recognise its beauty until I moved to Sydney and found that deep evening light was one of the things I missed most about my hometown.

The Hawthorn that I grew up in during the 1970s was not the exclusive suburb it is now, but it was comfortable. Its class structure could be traced, as it can in many cities, by the undulation of the land – the higher the elevation, the more affluent the inhabitants. Around my neck of the woods that meant Kew was the rich suburb. Richmond, sitting flat next to the river, was working class. Hawthorn, on the slopes down towards the Yarra and various tributaries, sat in between. The lower suburbs hugged the river, and the river attracted industry because its flow allowed factories and abattoirs alike to flush away their waste. So many abattoirs lined the banks of the Yarra and Maribyrnong rivers that at times they appeared to run with blood. (There is a violent poetry in this image of the river, and if you see an aerial photo of Melbourne's rivers, creeks, swamps and billabongs they actually look like arteries, veins and capillaries.) It was, of course, these low-lying suburbs that flooded most regularly as the Yarra pulsed in and out.

My years in Hawthorn were defined, as most teenagers are, by the school I went to. It's now known as Hawthorn Secondary College but back then it was called John Gardiner High School. Pastoralist John Gardiner had established his homestead – as well as a conflictual relationship with the local tribesmen – in the area in 1837. When I arrived there in 1975 there were only two years (7 and 8) hanging out in portable classrooms along-side the building site where the school was being constructed. I kept a diary through my first year of high school and retain a particular fondness for my entry of 11 November: 'Today the Prime Minister of Australia was sacked. Mum and Dad say it's the end of democracy as we know it. Janice and I smoked a menthol cigarette.'

The school was a product of the educational policies of Gough Whitlam's reign as prime minister. The principal from 1974 to 1984, Betna Dryden, commented that 'It is necessary to look back on what was happening in Victorian education in the early 1970s to understand the design and decision of the Gardiners Creek High School Planning Committee'. She pointed out that the aim of education was less the passing of exams than social development and student interaction, and that John Gardiner High School 'was at the forefront of changes affecting the education system throughout the state'. Even so, the design was being modified as the building went up, and the open-plan classrooms took on a more conventional air as walls were put in. It only took a few more years to iron out the unconventional behaviour of the kids that attended the school and the teachers that taught there.

One of the things that made John Gardiner stand out was that it was built among a high concentration of private schools — such as Scotch College, Trinity Grammar School and Methodist Ladies College — to give parents in the area who believed in state education somewhere to send their kids. John Gardiner was an attempt to challenge the paradigm, an attempt that has been steadily eroded by changes in educational policy, and the general shift to the right, over the last thirty years.

These days students who go to the school wear uniforms. We claimed we didn't believe in them, of course, but we had an informal one: Lee jeans, Miller shirts with lurex threads, and treads (heavy sandals that were made of ribbons of suede and had tyre treads for soles). In retrospect, this was a look that was heavily influenced by Melbourne's sharpie scene. The iconic photographer Carol Jerrems took her famous photos of sharpies around Heidelberg in 1974 and 1975. It wasn't easy work. After a film shoot, Jerrems said, 'I have myself only narrowly escaped rape but was bashed over the head by the main actor while driving my car, which had just been dented by the rival gang with sticks. They steal my money and cigarettes when I'm not looking, but I refuse to be deterred.'

The fact that the sharpie look reflected that of English National Front members at around the same time eluded me back then, but I find that disturbing these days. In 1975 many a lunchtime was spent in F5, one of the larger classrooms, practising sharpie dances to AC/DC. Melbourne comic Magda Szubanski, a former sharpie herself, has given many a fine rendition of these moves on both television and stage.

The school itself was a mix of the kids of lefties who felt they were making some kind of political statement by sending us there, kids who'd been chucked out of one of the aforementioned private schools, kids who were there simply because it was the local public school, and kids who'd recently arrived on boats from Vietnam. The result was an eclectic mix of class, ethnicity background and culture – a third of the students came from non-English speaking backgrounds.

I often think of the Vietnamese kids we went to school with and our absolute ignorance of what they'd gone through to get here, our lack of curiosity about the scars they bore. One boy had still-raw slashes across his face, another had clearly suffered malnutrition. Nam Le, the author of the 2008 short story collection *The Boat*, came to

Melbourne from Vietnam in 1979. He describes what these families were up against:

> My parents came here with nothing … And they just worked their butts off. They were working three, four jobs. They worked in manufacturing, they worked in retail, they worked in government, my mum was working in the post office for years and years, and so in one sense they were very, very concerned that us kids get the best education that we possibly could.

Many of those families moved to Richmond's Housing Commission flats – built at the same time as Fitzroy's. Footscray was another favoured location. The 2001 Census suggests that those families are, after 35 years, moving throughout Melbourne. However, Victoria Street, one of Richmond's main thoroughfares, is still an extensive and lively strip of Vietnamese restaurants, markets and shops scattered with small Buddhist shrines.

When we first moved to Hawthorn, my dad was an architect. Saturday mornings were sometimes spent at Bruce Weatherhead and Alex Stitt's Jigsaw Factory in Bridge Road, also in Richmond. The graphic design firm Weatherhead and Stitt put Melbourne on the map as a leader of graphic design – a title it still arguably holds. They'd designed forty-five different toys and games for the Jigsaw Factory. There was the Pirate Game, which my brother and I loved, Spellbound, and the maths game, Tableland, which we didn't love nearly as much. James Button was also a Jigsaw Factory aficionado and he recalls:

> Jigsaw had two doors: a normal one, and a tiny one for children. Inside, people who were small enough could crawl through wooden houses, giant snakes or a sunken toy pit, full of toys, beanbags and orange and purple cubes. Upstairs, Nancy Cato from the ABC's Adventure Island program ran theatre workshops, and Bruce Woodley from The Seekers would come in to sing on Sunday afternoons. But it never made money.

The Jigsaw Factory closed in 1973, after just under three years. A few years later I took to spending time in Richmond again, this time to see films at the newly opened Valhalla Cinema. Initially it didn't have seats so you'd take your own beanbag or, if you were going to, say, a 24-hour Woody Allen marathon, your own sleeping bag. Not only did the cinema show fantastic films, but it was also the perfect place for teenagers to pash. The Vallhalla went on to put in seats and become the home of two long-running audience participation films, *The Rocky Horror Picture Show* and *The Blues Brothers.*

The fancier suburb of Camberwell was to the east of Hawthorn, and while only 2 kilometres away it seemed like a different country. When the guinea pigs and rabbits I cared for at primary school were killed, we all blamed the 'Camberwell boys'. If they did exist, I assume one of the things that drove them was boredom: the entire suburb of Camberwell was a dry zone from 1920 until 2003, when a restaurant got a licence to serve alcohol. When I was a teenager, the Palace Hotel in Burke Road was seen as the last watering hole before one entered a terrifying wasteland of beautiful gardens, perfect hedges and no booze. But the suburb did boast the Golden Bowl bowling alley, which lives on in my memory as the place where boys I went to school with claimed — after she was in *Neighbours*, of course — to have got on with the area's most famous resident, Kylie Minogue. There was the very gorgeous Rivoli cinema, which was built in 1940, where I saw many a movie. There was the hardware store where my dad purchased what in retrospect seems like an inordinate amount of treated pine. Camberwell is still the home of a famous and long-lived flea market, which Michelle de Kretser often frequented. For Michelle, the market is a place

marked by impermanence. It materializes on Sundays from early until half-past noon. For those few hours, the workday parking lot between Burke Road and Market Place is reborn as an archive, a graveyard, a wonderland of desires … This is where you monitor the rise and fall of hemlines, this is where trousers first narrow or flare. The halter-neck maxi sashayed into view here at least two seasons before it swarmed over the chain-store racks. Ditto the quilted faux Chanel bag. Up and down the aisles strolls Melbourne style at its inventive, irreverent best. An old school tie does service as a belt, a 'do is adorned with a mauve plastic clothes peg … The toast rack [I buy] is for my sister, who collects Carltonware. When she heard I was leaving Melbourne, she said: 'But I always think of you at Camberwell market.' Today, along with these stalls, part of me is being dismantled. I tell myself I'll be back, as a ghost or a tourist.

In recent years, Camberwell was also the site of protests about the building of a multi-storey shopping complex over its railway station. Barry Humphries and actor Geoffrey Rush led an anti-development community march from Camberwell Junction to the station in 2004. The developer's plans were rejected by the Boroondara Council in 2009, but the Victorian Civil and Administrative Tribunal reversed this decision in 2010.

By the time Jeff and I arrived in Hilda Crescent, the agreed meeting point, I'd almost forgotten we were there to go draining. It was a bright sunny day, warm for winter, and going underground was more counterintuitive than usual. Hilda Crescent was one of the many Hawthorn streets that had its name changed at the outbreak of the First World War in an attempt to erase the suburb's German roots. Fritschs Road became Bowler Street, Weinberg Road and Grove became Wattle Street and Grove, Karl Street became Charles Street and Hildebrandt Crescent became Hilda Crescent.

Dougo walked towards us distractedly, staring mournfully at the ticket he'd received for driving while on his mobile phone. Despite the man's modest and laidback air, he's something of a folk hero. A few years ago, a sister organisation in France took him down into Paris's catacombs to a space as big as a ballroom where, as it happened, a masked ball was underway. While Melbourne does not boast Paris's hundreds of kilometres of underground tunnels, it does have Anzac, a cavernous drain under South Yarra where many parties have been held over the years. Other famous parties have been held in the Dungeon. The Dungeon's location – indeed the locale of all the drains where the Clan hang out – is a secret of sorts. When last I looked its website had been shut down, presumably because the Clan had been receiving unwelcome publicity. In July 2009 (a couple of weeks after I met Dougo) the deputy NSW state coroner looking into the deaths of two graffiti artists in a Sydney stormwater drain recommended the Clan be investigated. Hugh Dillon said he was concerned about the countercultural message of the group, which he described as consisting of 'shadowy characters'.

While there is nothing particularly shadowy about Dougo, it's true that draining is illegal. When asked in an interview for Melbourne University's *Farrago* magazine back in 2000 how the

Clan had such extensive knowledge of Melbourne's drainage systems, Dougo answered, 'Let's just say they [maps] were "acquired" and leave it at that'. The day we went underground the extent of our lawbreaking was some inelegant scrambling under and over wire fences.

I was right to be nervous, and not just because I no longer have the chutzpah of a teenager. Much as the Yarra claimed the life of John Batman's son some years after Batman gave the orders to dam its waterfalls back in the 1830s, so the drains around Gardiners Creek — concreted in and recoursed to accommodate a freeway — regularly take the lives of the kids that explore them. Our house in Hawthorn was near Gardiner Reserve, home to a concrete drain where Gardiners Creek used to run. On dry days we might play cricket on its bank, a bank also used as a place to make out — a kind of colonisation of the suburb by teenage hormones that I am slightly shocked to remember. (One of my first 'political' actions when I was head of the Student Representative Council at John Gardiner was to lobby for a 'kissing room' and David Nichols recently reminded me of hopes for the establishment of a smoking room. Both failed.) There were always stories of tough boys going into the drains, risking life, limb and a police record. Dougo, as it turns out, was one of those boys, though he's turned a teenager's love of adventure into something of a career.

Underground places, both fictional and real, are places of fascination. Think of the underground caverns of the Morlocks in H.G. Wells's *The Time Machine*; Londoners' retreat to the Tube system during the Blitz; the catacombs in Paris, millennia old and so extensive that both the French Resistance movement and the Germans bunked down during the Second World War without realising the other was there; the subterranean worlds of Manhattan's subway systems and the people who live in them, vividly captured in Colum McCann's novel *This Side of Brightness*.

The first thing Jeff and I learnt as we shimmied into an open drain and walked towards the square concrete opening that would take us underground is that a drain is not simply a drain. The various types include horseshoe, arch, bowl, mushroom, egg, pear, square, rectangular and square with pointed top. The central drain of the Maze is about 3 metres in diameter, cool and dry. I had expected it to feel closed in but it didn't, not at all. Nor did it smell of anything other than slightly stale air, and water. Tiny drains – no bigger than a hand span – led up to the surface at regular intervals, creating pinpoints of light. Traffic could be heard overhead – at least at the higher points of the drains. There were manholes leading to the street and shops above us. At some points the drain had been shifted to accommodate the foundations of new buildings.

Something about walking under a city brings out the history nerd in people, and moving slowly down into the tunnel system becomes a personal excavation of sorts. As you pass from modern concrete drains to bluestone cobbling and on into older, circular red-brick sections, you feel the passage of history and time. Dougo's passion for Melbourne's stories runs deep. If you count the number of newsletters he's produced on Melbourne's drains (newsletters on specific drains interspersed with more general local history), he's pulled together an amazing body of knowledge. Despite this, when asked what he did for a living he said, 'I'm only a storeman'.

The original sections of Hawthorn's main drain were built during the late 1880s. Earlier, waste from the earth closets that were used for toilets ran straight into gutters or the Yarra River whenever it rained. As a result there was a lot of typhoid and cholera. In its early stages, the main drain was an open-topped canal where the factories and drains that line Gardiners Creek dumped their waste. In 1888 a royal commission into public health in Melbourne led to the formation of the Melbourne Metropolitan Board of Works. For the next decade there was much bickering between the government, local councils and the MMBW. Sections of the main drain were built at different times, which explains why the tunnel is made out of a variety of different materials. While the sewer main was being constructed in Hawthorn, the creek was being converted to a stormwater drain, formally opening in September 1909.

This history lesson was delivered as Dougo strode ahead, confident over the uneven surface, while I scampered behind with my camera. The only light came from a couple of small torches and the occasional flash of daylight from points above us. The signs of human life along the way were graffiti and beer bottles shoved into nooks in the wall. We were walking towards Four Ways, a spot where four drains meet and art installations are scattered about. About a kilometre or so down the drain, the art began. There was Mickey Mouse, a tiny garden gnome, a shrine to what looked like a Wicca version of the Madonna, street signs, pictures of former prime minister John Howard and toy farmyard animals arranged in various lewd positions. Someone had painted 'my castle is your home' and it's true that these drains have the feel of rooms in a medieval keep.

There was something moving about the folk art, about the number of people who, free from the public's gaze, had chosen to make dioramas for all who followed them to see. Just as Dougo wouldn't describe himself as an 'explorer', these kids probably wouldn't describe themselves as artists, though there was a vitality and creativity on show, deep underground: things people might be embarrassed to do on the surface, they gave themselves permission to do here.

We kept walking until we ended up under an opportunity shop on Burwood Road. At that point there was a tag wall, which had been set up as part of the Clan's attempt to stop random graffiti through the tunnels. If the number of names on the board were any indication, dozens of people had made this place theirs over the years. When we looked up we saw the small hole drilled in the shop's floor. Apparently there used to be a trapdoor that allowed explorers to lift themselves up into the shop and have a look around. At some point, predictably, someone (not a Clan member) had trashed the shop and the owners had bolted the trap closed. 'Idiots', said Dougo, with appropriate contempt. As much as the Clan attempted to assert a kind of authority and code of behaviour underground, there were limits to how much control they could, or wanted to, exert.

Given our enthusiasm for the Maze, Dougo decided we were up to going down the Slide. This drain was tougher to move down. As with the Maze it was large, but there was a lot more water running through it, enough that you had to skip from side to side of the stream. Because of the curve of the walls, you had to move fast enough to keep your momentum going – otherwise you fell in. Dougo and Jeff skipped ahead of me with what looked like relative ease. I slipped and fell, but the whole thing was, frankly, such fun it was hard to care. After what felt like a couple of kilometres, the drain stopped abruptly and turned into a small waterfall, which fell down into a wider, squarer space, as big as a warehouse. It then narrowed dramatically and became circular again before flowing out into the Yarra.

We had to climb over a bar, scramble down a metal ladder and then drop onto the mossy drain floor, which was slippery like ice. This section of the drain was really quite beautiful, curving around so that you only got the view out into the Yarra at the last moment. It felt like a glimpse into another world, and I thought of the flash of parallel universes seen through windows in Philip Pullman's novel *Northern Lights*.

Perhaps it was no coincidence that the book I was reading that month was China Miéville's *The City and the City*, a futuristic novel in which one city is split into two through the existence of a kind of twilight space, one full of possibility but that also causes fear. Being in the drains was like being in a shadow suburb, one that had a relationship to the world up there (we were under Burwood Road, we were under the opportunity shop ...) but at the same time gave me a freedom I hadn't experienced when I was growing up in the streets above. In this and many other ways, going down the drains was like re-entering childhood and a kind of joy: we all seek out wild and secret places as children, but are more fearful about doing when we're adults. These hidden spaces remain compelling, though. They're challenging to get to, illegal to enter and private once you find your way into them.

It's true that familiarity inevitably breeds contempt, but it was something else about the suburbs. Is this a trace memory of the communities whose way of life was erased for us so we could live there – including the "'Aboriginal with a good reputation' in irons and severely wounded about the head' that one G.M. Langhorne found at John Gardiner's homestead one afternoon? Is it the knowledge that the people who were joining us in our increasingly multicultural city knew of things the very construction of the suburbs were designed to erase: the German-ness of Hildebrandt Crescent; the horrors that must have been endured by the young Vietnamese man who sat, with his face slashed, in my classroom back in 1975? There is always another history or a more private story underneath the public face of any city, of any suburb. But the centres of towns tend to be messy; it's harder to hide things, things that you can convince yourself aren't there in the polish of the suburb. Perhaps, down in the drains, there was the relief of not just sensing that, but knowing it to be true.

The Latin motto on Hawthorn's crest in 1860 was *Ex umbra in solem* – 'Out of the shadow, into the light'. The Aboriginal name for the area,

Boroondara, translates to 'place of shade'. When the Clan was naming this network of drains, Dougo argued for Boroondara rather than the Maze and the Slide. 'It's right, isn't it?' he gestured around the drain, towards the entrance and the sunlight that was glinting on the water. 'This is a shady place.'

On the first Saturday in August, Virginia and I walked into town. It was freezing and we were wearing the full winter regalia: beanies, scarves, mittens and heavy coats. August is our coldest month. In the face of such discouragement the culture ramps up, and it's at this time of year that both the Melbourne International Film Festival (MIFF) and the Melbourne Writers Festival are held.

The development of Melbourne's identity as a cultural and sporting event capital has been enabled by huge injections of cash over the last three decades, part of a strategy initiated by John Cain (who took office in 1982 and was Victoria's first Labor premier in twenty-seven years) in response to the deindustrialisation and decay of the 1970s. It was a strategy that gained momentum in the nineties, when Jeff Kennett was premier. It's been an extraordinarily effective way of creating employment and attracting tourism. And yes, it can make the city an energetic place to live. Key sporting events include the Australian Open tennis (January), the Formula One Grand Prix (March), the AFL grand final (September – rest assured that you'll be reading more on that) and the Boxing Day cricket test (December). The arts has the Comedy Festival (April), MIFF (July/August), the Melbourne Writers Festival (August/September) and the Melbourne International Arts Festival (October). Some days I think this is a good thing, and other days it seems a dilemma. To quote Hilary McPhee's *Meanjin* essay 'A Timid Culture': 'We now package crucial debates as public entertainment … Audiences are consumers rather than citizens, booking the sessions out, asking their questions, getting their books signed and going away until next year.'

There are smaller festivals too – ones that aren't a part of that major events schedule – such as the gay and lesbian Midsumma (January); the St Kilda Film Festival, the Emerging Writers Festival and the Melbourne International Jazz Festival (May/June); and the Fringe Festival (October). They're an important antidote to the homogeny.

MIFF's beginnings, it must be stressed, were not strategic, but controversial. That pattern has continued. The Australian Council of Film Societies held the first iteration of the festival in 1952, in Olinda out in the Dandenong Ranges. Sixty people were expected but 600 turned up. At the time the *Herald* mentioned concern about 'Red' influence, but decided that art had won the day. As Jeff and Jill Sparrow noted in *Radical Melbourne 2*, 'ASIO, however, knew better ... "The overall picture of the Film Festival appears to show that communists, communist sympathisers and communist organisations were very much in evidence."'

Ironically one of the controversies around MIFF in 2009 was the claim that the festival had undermined the Chinese government by screening *The 10 Conditions of Love*, a documentary about exiled Uighur leader Rebiya Kadeer. When the festival did not modify their program in response to this objection, their website was hacked twice: the first time to display a Chinese flag; the second to make it appear that all film sessions had been booked out, thus deterring potential patrons.

MIFF is Australia's largest and oldest film festival, and I was a regular attendee for ten years or so until the number of writers' festivals I had to attend for work broke my festive spirit. My mother bought me a pass to MIFF for my eighteenth birthday and I spent two weeks in St Kilda huddled in the Palais Theatre's cold and uncomfortable seats, quite transported. The experience was simultaneously the most solitary and social experience of my life – alone with my thoughts but in company. When I think back to those days they seem like some rite of passage into adulthood. The festival has roamed around several of Melbourne's significant old theatres. In 2009 the Forum on Flinders Street was home to the festival club and a number of screenings. It's one of Melbourne's more bizarre Neo-Gothic buildings, boasting a Moorish Revival exterior, Greco-Roman statuary and a sky-blue ceiling decorated with small twinkling stars. The Forum has had many lives: as a theatre, as a cinema, as a revivalist centre and now, when MIFF is not on, as a live music venue.

Virginia and I weren't going to the festival that day – we were heading to Idlewild Press in the Nicholas Building, where we were booked in for a letterpress workshop. So, we walked past the queues outside the Forum and went across the road to Federation Square to grab a coffee. Fed Square stands where the very unappealing Gas and Fuel buildings (the more common name for the Princes Gate Towers) once were. Those buildings, like Fed Square, had been intended to cover the Jolimont rail yards below them but the project had stalled. Even today, and despite recent development and impressive landscaping, the massive area of tracks where trains and an electrical substation are housed is an eyesore. It takes a great feat of the imagination to picture the land as it was: an enormous wetland fed by a stream that trickled down from Fitzroy Gardens before being absorbed into an area rich with bird and plant life.

If you walk down the steps on one side of Fed Square you are on the banks of the Yarra. It's an erratic river. One day its flow is slow and sluggish – it's been as low as 17 million litres a day – but during times of flood up to 97 000 million litres has coursed through its beds. It's during these regular floods that the river pushes out into tributaries and marshlands. This contraction and expansion is as regular as a long, slow heartbeat. It's what made fertile the broad flat plains that Melbourne is built on. As Kristin Otto wrote in *Yarra*, 'A time-lapsed, Bunjil-eyed view of the river over tens, hundreds, thousands of years would show a living thing expanding (flood) and contracting (drought), changing beds, looping cutoffs and billabongs running faster or slower, in different unpredictable patterns'.

The heart metaphor was taken up by Environment Victoria's spokesperson Leonie Duncan at the end of May 2009. Melbourne's dams were only 26.7 per cent full and a report had suggested more water might be extracted from the river – despite the stress the fires had put on it and the fact that it had been, at some points, recently running at about a tenth of its natural level. Duncan said that trying to wring more water from parched rivers was 'like going to someone who is hemorrhaging to ask for a blood donation'.

It's here, down by Fed Square, in the depth of winter, down by the Yarra, that I think of William Barak, a Wurundjeri-willam man, and one of Melbourne's great leaders. The Melbourne City Council has, in recent years, attempted to make amends for the Victorian government's refusal to contribute to a memorial to be erected in Barak's name after his death in 1903. They've done this by landscaping the area around the river bank, now known as Birrarung Marr, and naming the bridge that takes people across to the MCG from this point the William Barak Bridge. The area has several very striking artworks inspired by Indigenous culture, including a sculpture based on an eel trap. For those who haven't seen an eel trap they are sinuous coiled affairs, much like the eels them-selves. They were designed to capture the eels as they migrated up the river. The migration itself was an indication that the time had come to move to higher ground, in preparation for winter. Even today eels migrate up the Yarra from the sea, often finding their way along the various drains that feed into the river.

William Barak was with his father, an elder named Bebejan, at the signing of Batman's treaty. Barak's great-great-grand-niece, Joy Murphy-Wandin, who leads Welcome to Country ceremo-nies at most significant public events in Melbourne today, said of him:

> My great great uncle William Barak was at the
> signing of the calculated treaty with Batman,
> and I think of a boy of about ten years of age,
> standing proudly there at this moment … Maybe
> he was able to understand from that meeting that
> there was going to be a big change. Barak … was
> an educated man from the beginning, I think he
> knew about life and where it might go; he had this
> vision for the future.

As a young man Barak rode with the native mounted police. In 1863 he led a small group to Coranderrk in Healesville and established a community with the help of a white man, John Green. When the community started growing hops profitably, the misnamed Aboriginal Protection Board imported white workers and took the money: 'The Board is under no obligation to pay wages to the Aborigines … They must be attentive and civil to all persons otherwise they will be sent away.' Barak and his cousin Simon Wonga undertook a 60 kilometre march from the Coranderrk Estate to the steps of Parliament House to seek justice on this and other issues, but it was to no avail. In the 1890s the protection board decided that only 'full-bloods' could remain at Coranderrk, tearing the community apart. Both Barak's children died, and the death of his son, David, from tuberculosis, broke his heart. He spent his final years painting, bequeathing us an extraordinary record of both traditional and post-contact life as well as creating a powerful aesthetic.

Federation Square was commissioned in 1997, construction began in 1998 and it opened in 2002.

It's a fractious building – all angles, glass and stone – that houses the SBS offices and various cultural organisations such as the Australian Centre for the Moving Image and the Ian Potter Centre (the National Gallery of Victoria's gallery of Australian art) alongside bars, cafes and restaurants. Its large open area is where Virginia and I, along with thousands of others, watched then prime minister Kevin Rudd's apology to the stolen generations in early 2008. That was also the year the Melbourne Writers Festival took up residence, moving to Federation Square from the Malthouse Theatre in Southbank.

When the international competition to design Federation Square was won by a joint proposal from Lab Architecture Studio (then based in London) and Bates Smart, there was criticism of the decision to use largely unknown and untested architects. There was also criticism of the design. 'Why is there so much space outside?' asked Leon van Schaik, the then dean of Constructed Environment at Melbourne's RMIT University.

> Where these places work like Berlin, there is five
> times the density of population … Barcelona,
> 10 times the density of population. You have an
> open space in Barcelona, it is filled with people,

necessarily. They come out, they spend their evenings and they are chatting and talking. That's not the case in Melbourne. This is a city that covers six thousand square kilometres.

It's true that Fed Square has some problems. While the space that faces Flinders Street Station works, as does the esplanade along the Yarra, the side that faces Flinders Street has never come together. It feels grey and dark much of the time, windswept and cavernous. Several of the restaurants on that side have failed. But van Schaik has, by and large, been proved wrong and Fed Square is full most of the time. People gather there to do all kinds of things: look at art, line dance, attend protest rallies and watch events such as the soccer World Cup or Kevin Rudd's apology on its large screen. In winter there is often footage of a large fire flickering in a hearth, looming over the square's uneven cobblestones. This sounds like a cheap trick but it does actually work to suggest a place people gather. It even makes you feel warm if you stare at it long enough. As one of the lead architects, Peter Davidson, said:

> What we are trying to do is make a space of
> possibility. I think for too long architects have

tried to describe what the future would be rather than simply make a design that allows for possibility into the future. Buildings in many respects are like gifts, or public spaces are like gifts. You give them to the future.

After warming ourselves with coffee and the virtual fire, we left Fed Square and walked a couple of blocks along Swanston Street, towards City Square. When I was younger City Square was the place you went for protest marches. My parents were involved in the teacher union movement when I was young and it left an impression on me. One of my favourite photos of my dad was taken during Australia's first Vietnam moratorium in May 1970 when a total of 100 000 people marched along Swanston Street. Dad was carrying a sign that said 'Fighting for Peace is like Fucking for Chastity', a phrase that indelibly imprinted itself on my political psyche.

In the late seventies and early eighties I was involved in the nuclear disarmament movement and many of the rallies I attended began in City Square. My memories of the space are mixed. There was excitement at being in the company of thousands of like-minded people combined with bursts of fear on the occasions horses were backed into the crowd. City Square felt empty and pointless a lot of the time, but at these moments it sprung into its own, became a rallying point. At that time the square seemed to me like an eternal fixture, but that was youth speaking – in fact, it hadn't existed for long at all. The Melbourne City Council started buying up land near the Melbourne Town Hall in 1966 to create space for a central plaza, and many of the city's Victorian buildings and arcades were lost in the process. The Builders Labourers Federation put their foot down over the Regent Theatre in Collins Street and placed a green ban on it, preventing demolition. The Regent then sat empty for close to three decades, a fading symbol of the tensions between conservation and progress, before being returned to its former glory and reopened in 1999.

Perhaps because City Square was a latecomer to the CBD, it never really did belong. There were endless bungled attempts to make it feel more vital, and in the late seventies the then young architecture firm Denton Corker Marshall was commissioned to redevelop it. Their redesigned square was officially opened in 1980 and included shops, a water wall and a much-heralded sculpture called *Vault* that was soon, offensively, dubbed 'the Yellow Peril'. I liked the series of canary yellow planes set at odd angles to each other, but a lot of people didn't. There was a vehement campaign to have it dismantled. The council caved in after seven months and moved *Vault* to what historian Seamus O'Hanlon called 'the then-Siberian-end of the Yarra'. It now rests, fittingly, outside the Australian Centre for Contemporary Art in Southbank. ACCA itself is worthy of mention. Designed by Wood Marsh and conceived as 'sculpture in which to show art', its rusted brown metal walls are echoes of the warehouse that originally occupied the site. These days City Square (well, it's a rectangle, really) has settled down into a shopping plaza. People walk, shop, drink and eat there.

Memories of the arguments over *Vault* lurched back to life when the Melbourne City Council unveiled its new logo in late July 2009. It was a logo that, as design writer Elizabeth Glickfeld remarked, 'was instantly compared to the Melbourne City Council's most infamous and controversial commission from the 1980s'.

There was some justification for the outrage in that the Melbourne City Council hadn't asked even one of the more than 10 000 Melbourne-based design firms to pitch for the job. In the end the Sydney office of an international firm, Landor, designed the new logo. But while reaction to the logo was negative, it was often not clear whether the criticism was aimed at the logo, the fact it wasn't homegrown or the discipline of communication design itself. As Elizabeth Glickfeld wrote in *Meanjin*:

> One media personality thought it looked like a three on its side or 'a 1990s rave party'. Another person likened it to 'the Westgate bridge as it's collapsing'. Melburnians from all walks of life wrote in to the city's blogs and daily newspapers complaining of hypocrisy. 'What a disgrace,' wrote Olga Howell of Greensborough. 'So many talented local designers could have done as well or better. How generous people are with our money.' 'Hey, Robert Doyle,' wrote Alison Baker of Elsternwick, 'clearly you'd be happy your philosophy about having to go overseas to get the best doesn't apply to the selection of lord mayors.'

Finally we crossed Swanston Street to get to our destination for the day. The Nicholas Building sits on the corner of Swanston Street and Flinders Lane. It's an area that was once the centre of Melbourne's garment industry, or, as the people who worked in the lane described it, the *schmatte* trade. If

I were compelled to sum up Melbourne in a single building, it would be this one, with its striking terracotta and dark-green faience glaze facade. Once a building full of bootmakers, dressmakers and button makers, it's now an artistic hub and the place exudes an energy that is hard to replicate through organisation or force of will. If the Nicholas Building didn't exist it would be as if the city had lost a part of its soul. That soul is already in danger because it's not clear how much longer artists will be able to afford to work there, given recent rent rises.

Melbourne architect and urbanist Anna Tweeddale puts it like this when she spoke to Ben Eltham for a *Meanjin* article about the Nicholas Building's history: 'One of the things that is so special about a vertical space like the Nicholas space is the unplanned interactions that happen in the communal spaces, and that's very much the way that cities work, those unplanned interactions in the streets are really important ways of interchange and exchange'.

You enter the building from Cathedral Arcade, which acts as a laneway within the building, reflecting the streetscape that lies around it. It still has its original leadlight, barrel-vaulted ceiling

(Melbourne's first), complete with the glass chute that used to carry letters down from the floors above. There are three lifts – and this is the best thing of all about the building – two of which are staffed by Joan McQueen and Dimitri Bradas, the only two lift operators on the Liquor Hospitality and Miscellaneous Union's books. A third operator, Tim Fleming, is a working artist with a studio in the building.

Joan has been spending her days in her lift for thirty-five years, and its walls are covered with newspaper clippings and photos of children, grandchildren and animals. Some of the animals are her pets, others belong to building tenants. Joan's daughter operated the second lift until 2004. When she left, Dimitri took over. He once ran an art gallery in the building. He fitted his lift out with red velvet curtains and a stuffed bird he'd bought at the Coburg Trash & Treasure Market.

Eltham also interviewed Joan. She recalled:

> There was a theatre on the first floor, and it was run by brothers, you know, live theatre [she says with a wink and a flourish]. And they were like topless usherettes in there, so we used to be busy with elderly gentlemen. Then there was one of the girls, they were transvestites, I think, and anyway

one had a snake, she used to bring the round
basket in here with the snake in it.

She also had views on its present: 'There's more
artists, and also the graphic design more so these
days isn't it, they're all good girls and boys, and it's
nice to be with younger people'.

The bridge between the building's original
uses and the hive it is today, between the old and
the new, was the artist Vali Myers. Born in Melbourne, Myers lived in Manhattan's Chelsea Hotel
for many years before returning home in the 1990s
and starting a gallery in the Nicholas Building.
According to Dimitri, 'Once Vali moved in, every
other artist and his dog wanted to move into this
space, because I remember there were not many artists before she moved in, it was mainly craftspeople,
jewellers and the like'.

Joan and Dimitri only work during the week. So,
Virginia and I had to walk up the stairs to the sixth
floor to Carolyn Fraser's Idlewild Press, which was
one of several small presses that operate out of the
Nicholas Building. The studio sat at the back of
the building and opening the door was like looking
into another century. The space was dominated by
two printing presses: one a Vandercook (1968), the
other a Chandler & Price (1925) bought out from

Cleveland in 2004. That in itself was an achievement of some proportions. As Carolyn wrote in *Meanjin*:

> Uncrated, the Chandler & Price weighs 500 kilos. The Nicholas Building, also built in 1925, has a relatively small goods lift accessible off Flinders Lane. The lift is rated to 680 kilos ... Peter Horne, the boss, assures me that there won't be much buggerisation, and there isn't, until the last crate of the day. It makes it into the lift with a little clearance either side and Darren squeezed in front. This is our mistake. Darren is not a small man, perhaps 150 kilos. Perhaps had it not been the last crate of the day, I might have made the calculation in time, but didn't. It's subtle; a sudden jerk, then halt. Nothing. The grills are opened, slammed shut, the lever tried again. Nothing. The lift is broken: 500 kilos of press and 150 kilos of person inside.

It seemed somehow fitting that these remnants of America's print revolution had found their way to Melbourne, and not just because one of the city's first settlers, John Pascoe Fawkner, was a printer. Melbourne is a city that is both attempting to come to terms with revolutionary changes in the publishing industry and providing a home to many people dedicated to recovering, or working with, older technologies.

Alongside the presses, Carolyn had drawers full of type, most of which were purchased from printers in the American Midwest. Typefaces that she's salvaged include Kingspor Bros Orplid and sans serif mid-century-style advertising faces like Venus Extended, Spartan Black and Hellenic Wide. There are a couple of cases of wood type and a font of 96-point Century Schoolbook. Her house face is Van Dijk.

It was a demanding weekend's work. There was no heating, and for twelve hours on both the Saturday and the Sunday we hunkered down over our type sticks, wearing puffy jackets. We were taking good old-fashioned, full-of-pseudoephedrine Codral (not easy to find in the inner suburbs of Melbourne, I can tell you) in an attempt to keep the chest colds we were all suffering from at bay.

I, foolishly, planned to set several poems by Anna Akhmatova in 12-point Van Dijk. In the end I only managed to set 'Courage' and 'Your Lynx-Eyes, Asia'. Identifying each piece of type and then placing the tiny piece of metal in the stick is an incredibly labour intensive process. There used to be guys called swifts – 'on 19 February, 1870, George Arensberg, "The Velocipede", set 2064 ems of solid minion type in a single hour in an era in which 700 ems was considered average' – but I was not one of them. It took me all of Saturday to set around 150 words, and it took half of Sunday to wrap the small block of type I'd laid out with just the right amount of string so that the tension was correct and the type sat straight and inked evenly. Virginia was more sensible: she picked A.A. Milne's poem 'Hoppity', which gave her more space to experiment with graphic possibilities. She took the opportunity to use hand-cut wooden type blocks printed in three colours, each requiring a separate run through the Vandercook. As we worked away, with only the occasional soup break and the footy on in the background, I realised that I felt about as Melbourne as it's possible to feel. It was a good sensation, one akin to (but colder than) waking up and taking an early morning dip at Bondi Beach and consequently feeling very Sydney.

It is crucial that Melbourne find a way to continue to provide spaces for less corporatised forms of culture to exist. As Marcus Westbury wrote in a *Meanjin* essay titled 'Tiny Revolutions', in which he laid out the thinking behind his highly successful

Renew Newcastle project:

> From the commanding heights of global capital
> markets, the intimate spaces of our lives, our
> communities and cities are often invisible
> and imperceptible. Local economies and their
> possibilities are little more than decimal points or
> rounding errors. Their potential is easily lost in
> pursuit of the 'efficiencies' offered at the massive
> scale. Yet our cultures are resisting and shrinking,
> sometimes in defiance of but often in concert
> with the same logic and irresistible forces that are
> reshaping our cities.

The City of Melbourne benefits from the Nicholas Building, using it in promotions and claiming it as an example of the city's investment in art and culture. But the building's tenants have no protection at all. Rents increased by up to 40 per cent in March 2010. According to Dimitri: 'If you're a genuinely poor artist or architect or anyone, you couldn't afford to be in this building, because although it's still cheap, it's still a fair whack of money, so it tends to be people on the good side of precarious who choose to stay in this building'. By September 2010 the rent rise had forced Carolyn and Idlewild Press out of the building, which led to buggerisation all over again. When Carolyn finally left, a cabinet full of type fell over in the back of the truck, scattering type like so many breadcrumbs all the way from Swanston Street to the roller doors of Idlewild's new home at the Compound Interest, a warehouse in Collingwood established by designer Jeremy Wortsman.

My pleasure in building Akhmatova's poem using bits of wood and steel was not unexpected. It was something that had been on my mind since I'd seen an exhibition of hand-crafted books some twenty years ago. But my work life meant that I'd got bogged down in making books in the new-fashioned, increasingly digital way. As well, my focus had tended to the editorial side of things rather than production. Enjoying the pleasures of design, an object's history, had been more possible in my time at *Meanjin* than it had been for me in more mainstream book publishing. (There are, however, publishers – Penguin's Julie Gibbs comes to mind – whose attention to production and design detail within a mainstream house is extraordinary.) Working on the journal with designer Stuart Geddes and his small firm Chase & Galley was a real joy for this reason: his knowledge of the history of book design and typefaces really informed the editorial work I was doing and the kinds of essays I was commissioning at *Meanjin*.

Early Australian book publishing was centred in Sydney, around Angus & Robertson. But in the late sixties the Melbourne arm of Penguin Books, under publisher John Michie, made tentative inroads into publishing original Australian works. One of these was a volume of plays from the APG that included work by Alexander Buzo, John Romeril and Jack Hibberd. In 1970 Penguin also took it upon themselves to challenge the censorship laws, with the help of Philip Roth's *Portnoy's Complaint*. They printed 75 000 copies of that title in Australia, thus avoiding charges relating to 'prohibited imports', and distributed them around the nation before the police could do a thing.

Around this time Melbourne was developing the beginning of what has become a vibrant independent publishing scene. McPhee Gribble's rise in the late seventies and then its sale to Penguin in the early nineties reflected the rapidly changing landscape: the embracing of Australian voices by Australian readers followed by a rapid shift into globalisation and a more corporate publishing scene – which meant, consequently, a Sydney-centric one. Certainly by the time I was to work out at Penguin, in the early nineties, the drive up the Maroondah Highway to Ringwood no longer felt like heading towards a bohemia and the hills. It was more like being stuck an hour out of town and forced to buy potatoes in their jackets from the car yard next door for lunch.

Since then, Penguin has moved closer to the city. Independent publishing has re-established itself and includes publishers such as Scribe, Hardie Grant, Black Inc., Melbourne University Publishing, Text Publishing, Spinifex Press and Sleepers. Allen & Unwin's Melbourne office publishes a really wonderful children's list and their roomy terrace in East Melbourne was my home for a couple of years after I returned from Sydney. Not only do they produce notable books but they also include both staff and authors in weekly choir lessons (tuneless since birth, I declined to join them) and insist that everyone eat a lot of cake. The then senior editor, Andrea McNamara, used to bake for her colleagues birthday cakes that we all shared, cakes she felt reflected the personality of the birthday girl. I was very happy to be a mango tart and pleased also that my friend Susannah got to be a summer pudding. There was, however, a contentious carrot cake that the recipient felt was unwarranted.

The 2009 Melbourne Writers Festival opened on 21 August with a keynote speech by German writer Bernhard Schlink and the announcement of the *Age* Book of the Year awards. The winner of the fiction category was *Things We Didn't See Coming* by Steven Amsterdam and the apocalyptic subject matter of the novel certainly reflected the mood that had been hanging over Melbourne all year. A few nights later, Chloe Hooper's *The Tall Man* won the John Button Prize for political writing. Both books were written by Melbourne authors and produced by Melbourne publishers – Chloe's by Penguin Books and Steven's by Sleepers. Melbourne was pulling its weight again.

The city has always held its own when it comes to bookshops. In fact, it has more of them than anywhere else in the country. When Melbourne was young, most of these stores were based in the city or Carlton – in 1900 that small suburb had fifteen booksellers. It was in Carlton, too, that Readings, now one of Australia's best general bookstores, was born. Three days after the Melbourne Writers Festival opened, Readings turned forty and threw itself a party at the State Library of Victoria, complete with a particularly enormous chocolate cake. Ross Reading, his then wife, Dot, and Peter Reid (the perfect bookseller names) opened the store at 366 Lygon Street. It moved to another, larger, store in Lygon Street in 1983 and is now in larger premises again. Readings also has outlets in Malvern, Port Melbourne, the State Library, St Kilda and Hawthorn. The Hawthorn store was my first bookshop, which made it a first love of a special kind.

The public face of Readings, co-owner Mark Rubbo, spoke at the party. In 1976, when Rubbo bought the business with two partners, he was the owner of Professor Longhair's Music Shop on Lygon Street. Thirty-five years later he can still be found selling books in the Carlton store. Rubbo is also a major figure on the literary scene: in 2009 he was a player in Melbourne's successful UNESCO City of Literature bid, a judge of the Melbourne Prize for Literature and on the board of the then embryonic Centre for Books, Writing and Ideas.

Satirist Max Gillies was another speaker, and he talked at length about working in the fifties at Cheshire's of Little Collins Street, a shop that specialised in textbooks. There has always been an abundance of specialist bookshops in Melbourne. The most famous of these was Cole's Book Arcade, which was as much a circus as a bookshop and included both a menagerie and a mechanical hen. My paternal grandmother used to read me adventures called 'Boy Land', 'Monkey Land' and 'Pussy Land' from E.W. Cole's iconic *Cole's Funny Picture Book*, first published, in Melbourne, in 1879. Extraordinarily the book went on to sell a million copies, but I was oblivious to any notions of parochial pride — my grandmother taught French so I assumed Cole was from France. He was not French but he was both an eccentric and an entrepreneur. When he placed an ad looking for a wife, he asked that she be 'good-tempered, intelligent, honest, truthful, sober, chaste, cleanly, neat, but not extravagantly or absurdly dressy; industrious, frugal, moderately educated, and a lover of home'. Readers at Cole's Book Arcade were encouraged to sit and read in chairs, under signs that said: 'Read for as Long as You Like — Nobody Asked to Buy'. That's still a bit of a tradition at good bookshops around the place, and when I worked at Brunswick Street Bookstore a man came in with his son and read him instalments of Harry Potter most Sunday nights.

Entire communities grew out of some of the more specialist shops, as I learnt a few years ago when I was working on an article on Buddhism for *The Age* and interviewed Peter Kelly. He regaled me with stories of the Norman Robb Bookshop, where his friend Harold Stewart (a cohort in the Ern Malley literary hoax) set up a Traditionalist study group in the early fifties. The group – many of them architects – met in the shop on Friday evenings. After eleven years of discussing esoterica, they began to seriously practise religions as various as Hinduism, Catholicism, Orthodox Christianity and, in the case of Stewart, Buddhism. Kelly and several others became sufis and his descriptions of arriving in Pakistan in the sixties particularly charmed me:

> It was a major cultural shock! Particularly after all these high falutin conversations, in Collins Street, to confront India … Oh, it was unbelievable. And then when I went to Pakistan I went in the middle of Ramadan. It was unclear to me as to how much of this esoteric practice I was to take on. Whether

I was to go to a mosque five times a day and all
that stuff so it was all, so shall we say, I started
to lapse. Sufisim tended to be highly emotional.
What I needed was a cooler climate.

Kelly returned to Melbourne, where he went on to
work in publishing for many years and became a
serious practitioner of Buddhism. He has written
in detail about these years in a book that he self-
published in 2007, *Buddha in a Bookshop*.

Neither Cole's Book Arcade nor the Norman
Robb Bookshop exist anymore, but many others
have endured. These include the Foreign Language
Bookshop, China Books, Andrew Isles Natural
History Books, Books for Cooks, TS Bookshop
(esoteric), Golds World of Judaica, Hyland's (mili-
tary history), Metropolis (design and photography), Rendezvous (romance), Kill City (crime
fiction), Polyester (counterculture), Minotaur
(graphic novels, science fiction and comics), Collected Works (poetry), the Little Bookroom (kids)
and Hares & Hyenas (queer). There was a vibrant
radical bookstore scene, a tradition kept alive by
the New International Bookshop at Trades Hall
(a store managed by Jeff Sparrow in the early
noughties). NIBS is the descendant of the International Bookshop, the legendary left-wing book

retailer that operated in Elizabeth Street for many years and traced its lineage back to 1933. Study groups organised by shops like these resulted not just in talk but in serious political action.

The final speaker at the Readings party was longtime customer Helen Garner. She read an extract from her novella *The Children's Bach* that resonated with those who'd gone to Readings to find a house or housemate. The second store's large plate-glass windows were thick with ads, listing dietary and gender requirements of potential housemates, displaying little sketch drawings, and advertising rooms at what now seem like impossibly cheap prices:

> Embarrassed, they looked away at the windows
> full of white cards. 'There are some nice-sounding
> places,' said Athena. The girl was in a state. 'Yes,
> except this one,' said Vicki. She crouched down
> and pointed to a grubby notice right at the
> bottom of the mass. Athena bent over. 'To Let,'
> it said. 'One room, limited daylight only, $25 per
> week. NB house not communal.'

Garner's first novel, *Monkey Grip*, was published in 1976. While Melbourne was rapidly changing, the establishment was still stuffy — as headlines like this one from the *Herald* show: 'Head Prefect of Tammy Fraser's old school at the centre of a storm about junkies and the counter culture'. *Monkey Grip* was launched at McPhee Gribble's third lot of offices, in Drummond Street in Carlton, long before I worked there. Helen's main memory of the launch is of 'crossing that big front room and being buttonholed by [writer and former diplomat] Bruce Grant, who asked me sharply what the characters lived on … I don't remember much about the period but I recall a general feeling of benevolence extending from Mark and the shop in my direction.'

Monkey Grip went on to become Readings' all-time bestseller but has since been eclipsed by Christos Tsiolkas's *The Slap*. The two books represent a significant and symbolic cultural shift, from a straight Anglo Australian woman born in the forties to the gay son of Greek immigrants born in the sixties. When I interviewed Christos at Readings in November 2008 there were close to 200 people in the audience, the largest gathering I'd ever seen in the bookstore. I was finally getting the sense that a younger – though rapidly ageing – generation of writers and thinkers were being recognised.

The mood of the literary community at the

Readings party was complicated. On the one hand, there was genuine pride that four days earlier Melbourne had been declared a UNESCO City of Literature. On the other hand, the qualities that led to that designation were felt to be under threat: partly because of the Productivity Commission's recommendations that Australian publishers lose their copyright after twelve months but also because the digital age was beginning to shake things up as it had done with the music industry a few years previously. While the UNESCO designation and the Centre for Books, Writing and Ideas have real potential to enrich Melbourne's cultural life, this is only meaningful if that cultural life is genuinely flourishing. Otherwise, to get back to the image of the caged Coops Shot Tower, it simply fossilises.

So, here's the rub: Melbourne is a city that is building its reputation as a place where more independent, less corporatised forms of culture thrive. There are independent bookshops staffed by people who know their stock and have read the books they sell, pubs that have live music rather than being full of pokies, live theatre operating out of old buildings at the end of bluestone lanes, eccentric cinemas operating outdoors on rooftops, and old buildings with all kinds of eclectic businesses operating within their 140-year-old walls. Parochialism, which I used to consider something to escape from, has kept relentless and destructive change at bay in Melbourne. Tourism Victoria's ads capitalise on the city's olde worlde charms, and I assume they're one of the reasons why real estate prices are becoming so insane. This is a city you want to live in. The catch is, of course, that these products of olde worlde capitalism (small business, passionate entrepreneurs) do not operate as efficiently as the homogenous shopping chains and larger enterprises that characterise late-stage capitalism. But Melbourne stripped of its small enterprises, its eccentricities, its hidden places full of unexpected people and their eccentric enterprise — well, that Melbourne really would be a bleak city.

Spring

The Cape Lilac in our courtyard now looked as if it had been adorned with pale brown Christmas baubles. Its second common name, the Indian Bead tree, suddenly made sense: stick-like clusters topped off with marble-like balls that sit stark against the blue sky, graphic as a child's drawing. The balls are beige, but on the right day they look golden. It was spring, that in-between season in which the temperature lurches from frost one day to heat the next and it is almost always blustery. But that matters not, for September is really just a frenzied build-up to the last Saturday in the month, when the AFL grand final is held. Sure, footy is intense from March onwards: matches are screened on TV several evenings a week and on weekend afternoons as well; shows about the sport dominate the local television and radio; and on the weekends, it's impossible to drive through the inner suburbs of Melbourne without knowing what end of town a game is being played. Is it at the MCG (east) or Etihad Stadium (west)? Once you know that, you can start to figure out the consequences for traffic patterns — a complex form of maths at which most Melburnians are adept. But the traffic jams, the temporary ascension' of commentators to kings and footballers to gods, the endless Friday nights spent in front of the footy — none of it means a thing until finals time sweeps in on September's erratic gusts of wind.

You wouldn't (I didn't) auction a house in the last weekend of September, you wouldn't call an election, and even having friends over to dinner involves endless emails that go something like this — and here I quote James Button — 'Could we book in Friday September 10? I doubt if Geelong would be playing that night but if they are, we can change.' Etiquette dictates being provisional. As it happened, Geelong did play and the dinner had to be cancelled.

In 2007 I was so desperate to see Geelong win their first grand final in forty-four years that I paid $600 to sit in the very back row of the MCG. That's set back so far and high you're practically outside the earth's atmosphere. Stranger still, *I thought I was lucky!* The game was not close. Put bluntly, we smashed Port Adelaide. Pummelled them into the ground. But, like the nervous footy fans Matthew Klugman interviewed on the subject, I could barely bring myself to believe that victory was ours. As he wrote:

> Fresh memories of deceptive expectations can even lead barrackers to extreme denials of hope. In 2007 some Geelong followers provided an absurd example of this after the team almost lost the preliminary final they had expected it to dominate. Though Geelong led Port Adelaide by more than 60 points in the third quarter of the ensuing grand final, some Cats fans still refused to believe ...

After that glorious win in 2007, we lost the 2008 grand final to Hawthorn. But the stats were on our side. Geelong had transformed itself into one of the best teams of the decade, and, arguably, of the modern game. This success had thrown the team's fans and led to a profound reassessment of the Geelong persona. It was as if the eternally depressed guy at the party had become the life of it: dancing around the living room shaking maracas, the last to leave.

Football is important to Virginia and me. Our first what-I-can-now-see-was-a-date more than nine years ago was to a footy match. Virginia had turned up wearing a Geelong beanie, and if you're prepared to go on a first date wearing a beanie, you know who you are. That's an attractive quality. It wasn't long before I'd changed teams again, metaphorically speaking, and we were going out. When asked about our courtship, Virginia is always quick to point out that if I hadn't barracked for the Cats, we would never have become an item — and here we were, in 2009, lucky enough to be going to a grand final to watch our team play, for the third year in a row. But this time we were no longer the underdogs, and it was St Kilda that had been waiting more than forty years to win a grand final.

What is clearest in my memory of each of those three years is the half-hour walk from our house to the MCG. 2007 felt momentous and we'd walked to the G holding hands, with hope in our hearts. In 2008 we were nervous and Geelong was too. They blew it. We got sunburnt in the unseasonal heat, the MCG ran out of bottled water, and onlookers collapsed with a combination of nerves and heat exhaustion. 2009 was different again. The weather was freezing, and if the clock on the silo had been working, it *would* have said 11 degrees. Balls, and players, get bogged down on muddy days. The game is slower. Winning this final was going to require grim determination rather than speed. It seemed more important than ever that Geelong win, but given their exhaustion it was not clear they would. Both Virginia and I had too much understanding of the way history would remember the club if they lost two out of three grand finals. Instead of being the team that was dominant through the second half of the decade, they would have been reduced to the guys who were almost the best in the league but never quite had what it took.

It was a tough game and the first quarter looked bad for the Cats. The rain kept coming down and we all huddled in beanies and coats, clapping our hands together to keep warm — an extraordinary contrast to the heat of the year before. In the second and third quarters the game evened out. It became tough, dirty and akin to hand-to-hand combat. It was hard to pick the difference between the teams. At the beginning of the final quarter St Kilda were winning by seven points, but Geelong's Tom Hawkins landed a goal a few minutes in.

While it was another fifteen minutes before another goal was kicked, the battle for possession of the ball was so intense it was as gripping a quarter of footy as I've ever seen. 'The Saints defence are like men crazed', as one commentator said. The rain settled into a mist. The times when Gary Ablett Jr got the ball were, as always, extraordinary – he seemed to fly out of the pack of an ordinary game and transform it into something else again. When Geelong was two points behind and there were only six minutes to go, a string of passes between Joel Corey, Shannon Byrnes, Cameron Mooney, Paul Chapman and Max Rooke resulted in Rooke kicking the ball through the posts. St Kilda's Steven Barker flung himself at the ground, sliding along it until his head slammed into the post and touched the ball, reducing a possible six points to just one. The score was now St Kilda 67, Geelong 66. And then Joel Selwood kicked a behind for Geelong to even things up.

Meanwhile, in what seemed increasingly like a symbol for the tenor of the game, St Kilda's Brendon Goddard charged around the ground like a wounded bull, his broken nose strapped to his face with what looked like gaffer tape. Just as the game moved into time-on came the moment the entire game hinged on. Geelong's Steve Johnson had had a shocking day, but he spotted Ablett out alone and kicked towards him. St Kilda's Zac Dawson desperately smothered it, but Matthew Scarlett's inspired toe-poke off the ground put the ball into Ablett's hands. Ablett held on tight and raced down the ground, shepherded by Scarlett, then kicked the ball 80 metres. Travis Varcoe hand-balled to Paul Chapman, who snapped his third goal of the game. The score was now St Kilda 67, Geelong 73. Geelong supporters held their collective breath for the next few minutes as Max Rooke kicked another behind for Geelong and then Scarlett conceded one to St Kilda to bring the margin back to a goal. And then the siren went. The coach, Mark 'Bomber' Thompson, leapt onto his desk, Chapman leapt into the air and Geelong's players started rolling around on the ground together. In contrast, St Kilda captain Nick Riewoldt looked stony-faced and Goddard began to sob. For good measure, Rooke kicked an after-siren goal, making Geelong's winning margin twelve points.

We walked back 2 miles through Melbourne rain (but we could have walked 10 more). There may have been skipping. We didn't quote the poet Bruce Dawe but we should have, for he's a man who understands days like this: 'And the tides of life will be the tides of the home-team's fortunes/— the reckless proposal after the one-point win/the wedding and the honeymoon after the grand-final …'

It was hard for the world of books to regain my attention but I rallied. In early October, drinks were being held in town at the Hotel Sofitel, in Collins Place, for the short list of the Melbourne Prize for Literature. I'd been asked along because I'd had the imprecise role of advisor to the judges of the prize. Lazily, I caught the 112 tram the half-dozen or so stops to the top of Collins Street. (The hotel is high enough that you can, as a friend once did, wake to the sight of balloons floating past and tourists staring at you as you lie in bed.) I went up to the hotel's famous 35th floor, where you can see clear across the east and south-eastern suburbs of Melbourne; from the top end of town down to Elizabeth Street and back up to Docklands. The view from the toilets is even better.

The top end of town has not changed much in 170 years, except for the fact there are now buildings high enough to give me a vantage point. The building of Melbourne began in 1837, when, as Robin Annear describes it:

> gangs of convict labourers were put to the task of bringing Hoddle's grid to life. Armed with hatchets, they blazed trees to show the lines of streets and the position of allotments to be auctioned in the town's first land sale. Each of the grid's ten-acre blocks (except for those reserved for government use) had been divided into twenty half-acre (2000 square metre) allotments.

Those central main streets, known as the Hoddle Grid (west to east: Spencer, King, William, Queen, Elizabeth, Swanston, Russell, Exhibition and Spring; south to north: Flinders, Collins, Bourke, Lonsdale, La Trobe), were where the embryonic city lived its public life, a life crowned by Parliament House at the top of Collins Street, on Spring Street.

Collins Street was once the grandest shopping street in Melbourne and, as Graeme Davison has noted, the street's fortunes have long been a metaphor for Melbourne as a whole. It's still very lovely, though references to 'the Paris End' of the street are somewhat delusional, in part because of developments such as the Sofitel. Devised and planned in 1971, with soaring towers, a cavernous shopping plaza and heavy, uncreative modernism, it was one of several major developments that required the destruction of many of Collins Street's very elegant and, yes, Parisian-style buildings. As Seamus O'Hanlon points out in his terrific post-seventies history of Melbourne, *Melbourne Remade*: 'In many ways Collins Place was born old: state of the art in 1971, by the time it was finally finished it was already passé …'

Back up in the Sofitel, the speeches had begun. I took another champagne, moved towards the back of the room and continued my visual tour of the city: down Collins Street and across Swanston Street to Elizabeth Street. The overwhelming impression of early Melbourne, as imagined by any number of writers, including Peter Mews, is dampness:

> They walked a long block down Collins to
> Elizabeth Street. Here their progress was halted by
> a somewhat unpleasant watercourse which flowed
> the length of Elizabeth Street to the river …
> [there were] … two-storey houses on either side
> of the street, the privies of which were connected
> to cesspits that fed, by mistake or design, into the
> creek before them, itself feeding into the Yarra
> Yarra, from which the water was of course pumped.

On November 11 – lest we forget – I was back in town to hear the announcement of the Melbourne Prize's winners. This time we were meeting at Federation Square's BMW Edge theatre. I sat on the stage – one of an alarmingly long arrangement of judges, advisers and friendly sponsors – while the announcements were read, working on my public face, which I hoped expressed intelligent neutrality. There wasn't much else to do, really, and I felt like a total goose. Thankfully, the winners were more animated: Nam Le won the Best Writing award and Gerald Murnane won the Melbourne Prize for Literature.

In the half-hour I'd sat with my back to the theatre's jagged windows and the Yarra, looking up at the audience, I'd thought again about the fact that many of the writers we read now, were either born overseas or had parents who were migrants. Just to mention three: Nam Le was born in Vietnam, Peter Temple in South Africa and Christos Tsiolkas in Greece. It's hard to imagine the impoverishment of Melbourne's culture if we hadn't allowed the waves of immigration we've had since the Second World War. In December 1947 Australia's first Immigration Minister, Arthur Calwell, waited on Port Melbourne's Station Pier to greet a boat of refugees from war-torn Europe in a civilised image of welcome that now seems arcane. (Though it should also be noted that Calwell enforced the White Australia Policy.) In the twenty years thereafter 1 million migrants would land on Melbourne's shores. In 1966 alone, the number of migrants that arrived in a single year was more than 101 000. What would we be eating, drinking, reading? It didn't bear thinking about.

On the other hand, the senior writers were, like many Australians of their generation, and like me, descended from Anglo stock. Murnane is about as Melbourne as you can get: born in Coburg, he has barely left the city, let alone the state. He's a racing man and was accepting his prize just a week after the running of the Melbourne Cup, a race he'd written about most evocatively:

> Number fifteen *Tamarisk Row*, green of a shade
> that has never been seen in Australia, orange of
> shadeless plains and pink of naked skin, for the
> hope of discovering something rare and enduring
> that sustains a man and his wife at the centre of
> what seem to be no more than stubborn plains
> where they spend long uneventful years waiting
> for the afternoon when they and the whole of a
> watching city see in the last few strides of a race
> what it was all for.

In his acceptance speech that day Murnane told the audience that he hadn't entered himself into the prize in 2006 (that year the winners were Christos Tsiolkas and Helen Garner) because he would have been in danger of winning a trip to Italy: 'I have lived in Melbourne for forty-six years and have never felt like leaving; that seemed more like a punishment'. He finished his speech by reciting a list of all the streets and suburbs of every Melbourne house he had ever lived in. It had the redolent seriousness of a litany, and Murnane sounded like the Roman Catholic priest he had briefly considered becoming. Literature, like footy, does have its spiritual moments.

It was hoped that the wide streets and large lots that formed the Hoddle Grid would prevent slums. Samuel Perry, the deputy surveyor-general of New South Wales at the time, advocated strict adherence to Hoddle's layout and warned that any subdivision of lots or development of unplanned paths would mean that 'the houses will be huddled together, so as to impede a free circulation of air ... and Melbourne will be ruined before it has risen to maturity'. He was ignored, of course, and by 1895 there were almost three hundred lanes. The major laneways alternated with the larger streets and were named, somewhat unimaginatively, Little Lonsdale, Little Collins, Little Bourke and Flinders Lane. After that, names tended to fall away altogether. There were laneways off laneways. And laneways off those. How that played out is neatly Freudian – a metaphor built of bitumen and bluestone, in which the conscious (the grid) tried to repress the subconscious (laneways). Certainly it was in these laneways, as Perry predicted, that Melburnians indulged their more private behaviours: where they defecated and urinated, fucked, played, worked and drank. Brothels lined Little Lonsdale and gambling dens thrived in Little Bourke Street – the area where the Chinese, who began to arrive in large numbers during the gold rush of the mid-19th century, were relegated. Flinders Lane, however, was industrious in its pursuits and quickly established itself at the centre of the clothing trade.

And the subconscious has won, really, as it often does: Melbourne's new-found vitality is not the result of grand property developments – those modernist shopping plazas like Collins Place, devoid of light and oriented away from the street

— but in the revival of those narrow lanes, where money fell through fingers like water and shit once sat in buckets. O'Hanlon again: 'what has worked to enliven the city has been small-scale rather than grand, quirky rather than rational, and perhaps most importantly, local rather than global'. The laneways languished for most of last century, only to be rediscovered as the century drew to a close. Since the early nineties the laneways have become filled with nightclubs, clothes shops, jazz bars (the star is both located in and named Bennetts Lane), stencil art, restaurants and clubs. The earliest enterprise, one that pre-dates the laneway's refashioning, was the Italian Waiters Club in Meyers Place. Opened in 1947, it was a place for Italian and Spanish waiters to wind down after work. It was also known as a place you could get a drink after six o'clock closing, albeit in a coffee mug. The availability of illegal booze was one of the reasons the club used to be unmarked and you required a password to ascend the rickety wooden stairs. The interior decor stopped evolving around the 1970s, but you can still get a bowl of spaghetti and a now-legal carafe of wine for the retro price of $15. Once unique, places like the Waiters Club are one of dozens of places you can eat off the grid. Indeed some lanes, such as Degraves Street, off Flinders Lane, are one long stretch of tiny eateries where dumpling bars merging into focaccia places rubbing up against juice bars.

It was next to the Waiters Club, in 1993, that the first of the new wave of bars was built. Meyers Place was the first bar to take advantage of changes in the liquor laws that had been pushed through to enable Crown Casino's drinkers. It was also outfitted by the young Melbourne design firm Six Degrees, a firm that tended towards low-key fit-outs using salvaged materials. It's a look that has gone on to define what may be described as a Melbourne aesthetic. Simon O'Brien, one of the Six Degrees team, said:

> I think it's very important to preserve texture in the city … a European city is a collage of many different eras, and I think the problem that you get with a developer mentality or a clean slate mentality is that … you have to actually wipe the slate clean and then start from there. Whereas, in fact, you know, like, all the little eddies and pockets and textures and, you know, sort of the accidents of meshing things together are often a lot richer.

Six Degrees is also responsible for a number of other bars, restaurants and hotels around Melbourne, including Wall 280 cafe, in Balaclava, which was my local for a couple of years. It's a cafe with a cubbyhouse feel and good pide. Peter Malatt, another member of the firm, made sense of Six Degrees' approach this way:

> Most of us went to uni and lived in terrace houses
> in the inner suburbs … we're interested in that
> idea of compressing the entrance so when you did
> come in you weren't coming into a big wide space
> where everyone else was looking at you. You know,
> it was a little narrow entrance that you could
> sneak through without everyone being checked
> out.

It's in the laneways – particularly Hosier Lane – that you find much of the CBD's stencil art and graffiti. According to British street artist Banksy, 'The Melbourne graffiti scene has always been fiercely independent – it's confident in itself and it isn't chasing some 1970s New York idea of cool … I doubt it's something the authorities are particularly proud of, but Melbourne street art leads the world.' In 2003 Banksy stencilled a rat above a doorway in Hosier Lane, at the rear of the old

Russell Street Theatre. Most of the buildings in the lane have permits allowing street art, which naturally begs the question of whether graffiti is still graffiti if it's subjugated to such bureaucracy. The back of the old Russell Street Theatre didn't have a permit so abstract arguments about 'respect-able' graffiti and the nature of ephemeral art were somewhat dramatically resolved in mid-2010 when Banksy's rat was erased by a council worker who'd been told to clean up the lane and — well, so the media said but it seems too good to be true — 'get rid of the rats'. Melbourne City Council chief executive officer Kathy Alexander said that the council needed to implement 'retrospective legal street art permits' to ensure other famous or signif-icant street artworks were protected, but it's hard to imagine that a 'retrospective legal street art permit' will add substantially to Melbourne's street culture.

The artists who once worked in the odd little spaces in lanes off lanes are being cleaned up too — by rising rents. Even local and focused develop-ment has a gentrifying effect, and the artists who once occupied Fitzroy's and Carlton's nooks and crannies before moving into a depressed CBD are on the move again. Warehouses from Collingwood to Northcote to Preston are filling up with galleries, cafes and studios, and a substantial number of artists have given up on the city altogether and are moving to Castlemaine, 90 minutes north of Melbourne.

In a way that's as it should be. The art scene in Melbourne was born in then rural Box Hill in the 1860s, then moved up the road to Heidelberg over the next few years. It was Heidelberg that lent its name to the group of artists including Tom Roberts, Frederick McCubbin and Arthur Streeton. These were the first painters to come to grips with the sometimes harsh, sometimes gloomy light in the bushland of south-east Australia. Their rendering of light meant that the Heidelberg School artists were described as Australian Impressionists – a descriptive that tends to colonise the uniqueness of their achievement.

Modernism was born a few kilometres further out again, in Bulleen, among the linked lagoons known as the Bolin Bolin Billabong, where the Wurundjeri once fished for eel. It was here that John and Sunday Reed bought the Yarraside dairy farm in 1934. They lived there, first in the renovated farmhouse and then in a modern home the Reeds commissioned in 1963 (these are now the gallery spaces known as Heide I and Heide II respectively at the Heide Museum of Modern

Art), until Sunday's death in 1981. Both John and Sunday were fans of the Heidelberg School and they owned several works by family friend Arthur Streeton, who had painted Sunday as a young girl. More influentially, though, they were great patrons of contemporary Australian art.

Like the Nicholas Building, like the Last Laugh, but perhaps to more focused effect, the buildings at Heide (which include the more recent Heide III) are a crucible for a distinctively Melbourne scene. In the forties and fifties there was no Melbourne art story that did not, at some point, touch on the life of this place: one of grand passions, great paintings and terrible tragedy. Paintings including Nolan's Ned Kelly series and artists of the calibre of Albert Tucker, John Perceval and Joy Hester were nurtured there. These days the place gives shape to, and a focus on, their legacy. Their power would be somehow dissipated if Heide did not exist.

In October 2009 I visited Heide with Carolyn Fraser and writer Maggie Mackellar after we were on a panel together at a small writers festival in Eltham called World Matters. Heide III was between exhibitions so there wasn't much art to be seen, but the whole place is a work of art in itself. Sunday Reed's legacy is as much about her gardens, which include the heart garden (the memorial she created to her former lover Sidney Nolan after he had left Heide) and the kitchen garden (from which Sunday produced meals for all that stayed there). We paid homage to the kitchen garden, which was in need of weeding and water. You tread through it somewhat gingerly these days as there is a large sign when you enter telling you to look out for snakes. We checked out the open-air cat run, built alongside the original house for Sunday's Siamese; we walked down to the creek and looked for, but failed to find, the 300-year-old scar tree. Finally we visited Heide II and I showed Carolyn and Maggie what is called the living room but is more a pit with an open fireplace to one side. The couch and floor are covered in a continuous run of natural dark brown wool: a kind of furry modernist womb. It's my favourite room in Melbourne.

Heide's painters were known as 'Penguin painters' and they fought against conservative styling while being strongly influenced by early European expressionism and surrealism. There were Penguin writers too, including Geoffrey Dutton and the young poet Max Harris. The latter set up the magazine *Angry Penguins* in Adelaide to promote these new experiments in style and soon the Reeds were financing the magazine and editing it alongside Harris and Nolan. Some critics objected to their move away from classical values; others, like those of the Jindyworobak movement, sought to free Australian art from the 'pseudo-Europeanism' of its key influences. In retrospect Harris concedes, 'There were excesses, absurdities, and intolerable posturing among the Angry Penguins; and they were manifested by people like myself and Nolan and Tucker, leaders of the movement'. It was these excesses that led to the Ern Malley hoax – a prank that impacted on the culture in ways that the instigators, James McAuley and Harold Stewart, could never have imagined.

Ern Malley's 'poetry' was sent to *Angry Penguins* in 1943 by his 'sister', who said she sought to memorialise her now dead brother. Malley was, of course, a fiction, intended to highlight the pretensions of modernism. Harris fell for the gag, declared Malley a genius and published his work. 'Malley' was put on trial for obscenity (with Harris liable as publisher), and that trial added to the absurdist dimensions of the whole affair. Here's Text Publishing's Michael Heyward on the subject:

> [Detective] Vogelesang's evidence under cross-examination by Millhouse was a sensation. He

brought the house down … Meanings budded, flowered and died. If Ern Malley was written to be misread, no one had misread him like this. In 'Sweet William' Vogelesang objected 'to the thing as a whole', he said. 'The last five lines of the first verse are suggestive of sexual intercourse and the second verse is suggestive of the person or whoever it is having yielded to the temptation of sexual intercourse.'

None of this was the intention of the hoaxers. Indeed the drama so distressed Stewart that he withdrew from public literary life and in 1963 moved to Japan to practice Buddhism. McAuley, less repentant, went on to become the first editor of *Quadrant*, a magazine founded in 1956 by the Australian arm of the CIA's anti-communist organisation, the Congress for Cultural Freedom. The personal views of the authors became irrelevant as the poems took on lives of their own and became a flashpoint for the culture's unease, for Australia's attempts to break free of its history as an English backwater. The battle would keep on rolling until Tim Burstall's films and Penguin's publication of *Portnoy's Complaint*, but these first attempts to argue against parochial notions of decency were fuelled, no doubt, by a very different and much more indecent kind of war – the one being fought in the Pacific and around the world.

Harris was humiliated and McAuley and Stewart's mocking of modernism set the movement back some years. You can read this backtracking, this loss of confidence, in the pages of *Meanjin* and other journals at the time. Stories and poems were written with a cleaner, more powerful sense of possibility in the early forties, only to have the old guard reassert itself by the end of the decade. Did the hoax set the written word back twenty years? Some have argued it did. Others are less convinced. Heyward again: 'Was the hoax so influential in itself as to suppress an entire trend in contemporary Australian poetry, or was it that the guardians of the flame, who fought tenaciously for the qualities they wished to preserve in poetry, were among the strongest poets in the country anyway?' Poets still dispute James McAuley's claim that Malley's poems were 'concocted nonsense'. Judith Wright points out that the poems were 'a good deal better than true hoax poems need be'. I suppose, to get back to Banksy, when is a rat art? When is art ratshit? What are its political possibilities?

Melbourne's famous, quasi-legal stencil art scene

vaguely continues the spirit of Malley's provoca-
tions, but the local art world's most spectacular, and
explicitly illegal, political act was the 1986 theft of
Pablo Picasso's *Weeping Woman* from the National
Gallery of Victoria. This was only eight months
after Patrick McCaughey, the director of the NGV,
had paid a then record $1.6 million for it.

McCaughey is a Melbourne story himself.
Generous of spirit, fabulously scathing, a member
of Melbourne's establishment (his father, Davis
McCaughey, was a Presbyterian minister, deputy
chancellor of the University of Melbourne and
the governor of Victoria from 1986 to 1992) and
generally over the top, he's one of the few people I
know who can get away with pronouncements like
'We live in a philistine nation but a civilised city'.
He was the foundation professor of Fine Arts at
Monash University (aged 31) and was already a
legend when I joined that department as an under-
grad, partly because of his lectures and partly
because of the seminal book he'd written on the
Melbourne artist Fred Williams, an artist whose
work transformed the way we looked at Australia's
landscape. McCaughey was also *The Age*'s art critic
for many years. He left Melbourne in 1988 to run
the Wadsworth Atheneum, in Hartford, Connect-

icut, and later the Yale Centre for British Art. Back in 1986, though, he was dealing with the fact that thieves had walked into the NGV on a Saturday night, unscrewed *Weeping Woman* from the wall and walked down the corridor, unpicking it from its frame as they went. It was a crime that mimicked the way *Mona Lisa* was stolen from the Louvre in 1911. Both the homage and the finesse with which the painting was stolen suggested the culprits knew about art and art history. To complete the job they'd stuck a fake card into the spot where the painting once hung, claiming the removal was routine. This meant that it was more than a day before the theft was even noticed.

Not that the robbers wanted to go unnoticed. They sent letters addressed to both the Victorian government and the Minister for Arts and Police, Race Mathews. 'Attention, RANK Mathews', the first letter began. 'We've stolen the Picasso as a protest against the niggardly funding of the fine arts in this hick state and against the clumsy, unimaginative stupidity of the distribution of that funding.' If they didn't get the money, the painting would be burnt. They signed themselves 'Australian Cultural Terrorists'. Their logic was, I suspect, that spending so much on a single piece of art was a misuse of public funds when artists struggled to survive, but in the circumstances that argument wasn't going to fly.

A break in the case came when McCaughey received a call from art dealer Anna Schwartz (now the director of Anna Schwartz Gallery). She directed him to a young artist who'd been 'talking'. McCaughey headed off with artist and gallery trustee Jan Senbergs, looking, according to Senbergs, like 'a couple of sort of pseudo detectives'. Or, perhaps, like Detective Vogelesang. Two days later Margaret Simons — a prominent Melbourne writer and commentator who was then a journalist at *The Age* — was told to follow up an anonymous call that suggested the paper 'look in luggage locker number 227 at Spencer Street Station'. Simons did look in luggage locker number 227, the painting was there, undamaged, and champagne corks were popped — but the identities of the Australian Cultural Terrorists were never discovered. The whole thing was like a plot from a Shane Maloney novel and it in fact became one, providing some inspiration for *The Brush-Off*.

The art scene in Melbourne today is supported by dozens of galleries that start in Flinders Lane but spread through the CBD and Melbourne's suburbs. There are several significant institutions: the

Australian Centre for Contemporary Art and the NGV at Southbank; the NGV's Ian Potter Centre, which specialises in Australian art and includes a strong collection of Aboriginal work, in Federation Square.

Much of the work currently being produced in Melbourne is – as it is elsewhere – installation-based, though according to several curators quoted by Justin Clemens in Spring 2009's *Meanjin* Melbourne's artists 'do everything'. This fact, and the consequent problem of how to judge work that is so multifarious, led to some debate on *Meanjin*'s blog. It was a debate that, tellingly, harked back to the Angry Penguins several times, circling around the issue of whether contemporary art (or conArt, as W.H. Chong called it) today is as radical and angry, as *meaningful*, as the Angry Penguins were in the 1940s. And so we're back to that mirror ball and its energising, infuriating, refractions.

I get to see most of my art these days at dawn, in a light that is not so much refracted as tremulous and breaking. My yoga classes are above an artists' collective, Gertrude Contemporary, and I often stand there for a minute or so and look in the front window at the revolving series of installations: blow-up dolls and castles; haunting sounds;

bird cages; disused machinery; paintings evocative of the sea; or, memorably, holes cut into the floor boards – the suggestion of hidden spaces, of space full of emptiness. (Fitting, I'd think, as I headed upstairs to meditate.) Gertrude Street also holds an annual projection festival. The flickering of a tree made of light is haunting, swaying back and forth on an imaginary breeze on the side of old buildings – the ghosts of trees that once grew in this bitumen and bluestone suburb.

There's a lot of stencil art and graffiti in and around my street as well. It's vibrant and various. There is the glorious, finely detailed fallen angel; the sloganistic ('Touch This Space For Financial Freedom'); the whacky (usually robotic); the lazy (a drunken burst of spray paint) and the eighties-style homages reminiscent of the great American artist Keith Haring – who, incidentally, has a mural on the wall of the old Collingwood Technical College, a kilometre or so east. It's one of the only remaining Haring murals in the world and has been there since 1984. It's now in a state of some disrepair. There is also the occasional installation piece. My favourite – until it was prised from the footpath – was the impressive concrete replica of a Nokia mobile phone that sat by a fire hydrant. On its tiny screen, in a classical typeface, the artist had carved: 'Fuck Art'.

At the beginning of 2009 I'd scored an unlikely gig with the unlikely title of 'ambassador' to Hilton's new hotel at South Wharf. *Meanjin* interns and other friends had more access to martinis and tapas than they might otherwise have had, but it also gave me the opportunity to watch an area that had been rundown wharves and a single exhibition centre evolve into a precinct that drew crowds along the river from Southbank and Crown Casino and become a lively area in its own right. The last time I'd spent time there had been in 2002, for the short-lived Melbourne Music and Blues Festival. Then the area had been a dusty, windswept space that was only just compensated for by having Ray Charles, Wilson Pickett and Bob Dylan on the same bill.

Things had changed. On higher floors of the Hilton the rooms have 180-degree views, and if you look east up the Yarra, towards Southbank, you see a pretty series of footbridges, criss-crossing the river all the way to Princes Bridge. If you look west you see the West Gate Freeway, the Bolte Bridge and an expanse of suburbs that stretches out from Footscray and Yarraville towards Sunshine. Directly below the hotel a shopping centre that we dubbed Big Land became bigger by the minute, as if someone had just got a giant new Lego set to play with. You also had your sleep punctuated by regular bursts of flame that shot up outside the casino in a display of Las Vegas showmanship that was slightly nauseating, and especially if you thought about the number of birds that the flares kill. I recently rewatched *The What If Man*, a documentary made about the life and work of my biological father, science fiction expert Peter Nicholls. Much of it was shot in this part of the city. In it Peter speaks of the way Melbourne, like many other cities, is trying to project an idea of itself as a city of, and for, the future. The cheesy theatricality of the flares were a way of giving the city a *Blade Runner* touch.

Much of the development in the south of the city took place in the 1990s, during the reign of Jeff Kennett. The Melbourne Exhibition and Convention Centre (designed by Denton Corker Marshall) next to the Hilton is known colloquially as 'Jeff's shed' and it is an elegant piece of design. The football stadium in Docklands – once known as Colonial

Stadium and Telstra Dome and now as Etihad Stadium – is much used, if not much loved ('Everybody slips at the Dome', as the Coodabeens sing). Crown Casino was the most controversial development of Kennett's seven-year term. The complex cost $1.85 billion to build and there were allegations of corruption in the tendering process. There was also concern about the moral dimensions of gambling. The casino has proved to be such a money spinner, however, that neither political party is interested in harking back to the good old days when the state didn't have one. What most people remember these days is that actor Rachel Griffiths protested bare-breasted at the casino's opening in 1994.

Melbourne's earliest burst of development began in 1854, and it too was fuelled by gambling: the rush for gold. Train lines unfurled with the speed of a pumpkin plant throwing out its tendrils. By 1884 this development was formalised by the *Railway Construction Act* (known as the Octopus Act), which authorised the construction of a further sixty-six lines. That amounted to almost 900 miles worth – more than twice the length of today's rail system.

In 1929, more suburban trains left Flinders Street Station in peak hour than do now, they were more likely to be on time, and the city was considered to have one of the best railway systems in the world. The lines dictated the shape Melbourne took and encouraged an easy relationship between the centre of Melbourne and the (retreating) rural landscape around it. Eventually Melbourne followed the tentacles of the railway line south and along the coast, as well as north to Coburg and east and northeast to Hawthorn, then Camberwell, Lilydale and, finally, Healesville.

The speed of this growth indicated two tendencies already apparent in the brash young city: one being a desire to sprawl ever outward, and the second to be a city with plans bigger than its relatively small population could sustain. Not all of these lines had enough customers to keep them going. The inner circle between Royal Park and Fitzroy and the line from Epping to Whittlesea no longer exist. Another extinct line, known as the Outer Circle, went through suburbs including Kew East, Camberwell and Burwood and then out to Oakleigh. These disused lines still snake through the suburbs and many of them have become walking tracks and bike paths.

The size of our population was not the only reason the system began to shrink. Melbourne, like most cities in the last century, began its love affair with the car. By the 1970s, the rail system was in deficit. In the 1990s the Kennett government attempted to deal with this through a combination of unwise service cuts and genuine efficiency improvements, and then in 1999 privatised the entire public transport system. That's when, according to Paul Mees, a senior lecturer in Transport Planning at RMIT, 'remaining skilled staff left, while labyrinthine contractual and administrative arrangements created confusion instead of accountability.'

Melbourne's trams were affected as well, when looming privatisation led to the removal of their conductors in 1998. In the twelve years since Melbourne's tram conductors were last active, their sense of humour and customer care has been somewhat mythologised, but there is no doubt that passengers liked to chat to them, were more likely to pay their fares and felt safer with them around. Certainly my parents were happy for my brother and me to travel on trams when we were young kids because there was a sense we were being watched over. While I wasn't one for a long conversation on the trams, I always admired the conductors' old brown leather ticket pouches and their nifty hole punchers.

These days, those who still call themselves conductors describe themselves, and their skills, 'as critically endangered alongside other Australians like the Orange-bellied Parrot'. Some of them have kept the tradition alive by occasionally conducting trams in India for the Calcutta Tramways Company. There are still calls to return conductors to trams, partly because the ticket inspectors who replaced them have abandoned the whole dealing-with-the-customers-with-a-sense-of-humour business. As Luke Williams outlined in *Crikey* towards the end of 2009:

> Complaints about authorised officers nearly
> doubled in the past 12 months and have
> increased every year for the past five years. Of the
> complaints, 31% were about intimidation, 22%
> about the use of force, the rest were largely about
> officers not listening or acting aggressively. One of
> the biggest causes for complaint was that officers
> travel in groups of up to eight and stand in a
> circle around people if they don't have a ticket.

The fact that it would, by some calculations, only take $20 million or so a year to reintroduce conductors makes the new Myki ticketing system seem particularly misjudged. Overseeing the new ticketing system became Lyn Kosky's job when she took on the role of Minister of Transport and the Arts (now doesn't that portfolio sound like something out of a Shane Maloney novel) in 2006. Myki has ended up costing $1350 million (compare that to Perth's fully functioning $35 million SmartRider ticketing system). While Myki was due to be up and running by the end of 2009, it finally kicked in across bus, tram and train in mid-2010.

Trams don't cover as much ground as trains but they have maintained customer loyalty far more effectively. The first trams were horse drawn, then there was cable, and by early last century they were electric. I like to think the ongoing use of W-class trams ('green rattlers') has contributed to their popularity. They were ubiquitous from 1923 until well into the eighties and some still run on inner-city routes today. As well as being more open to the air and having wood panelling, the W-class trams make a particularly satisfying ding when you pull their leather cords.

Because I lived in Fitzroy, I was a fan of the tram rather than the train. When I was a student at Monash Uni, though, the only thing to do was to get in my 1963 Holden (purchased for $100) and head forty minutes up the half-built South Eastern Freeway. The alternative was catching buses that would have taken close to two hours each way. Over the five years I attended the university there was much talk that a train station would be opening any minute. As transport plan after transport plan continued to focus on freeways rather than public transport, both Monash and Tullamarine Airport have been forced to rely on buses while waiting for those promised railway lines to be built. (There are rumours of a secret railway station that already exists under the airport. I couldn't substantiate those rumours but I was led to many a weird conspiracy website in the process.)

In 1969 several US engineering consultants came to help develop a transportation plan for Melbourne. They proposed a grid of freeways placed over the entire metropolitan area, much like in Los Angeles. Around the same time the Melbourne and Metropolitan Board of Works and the Country Roads Board were setting aside large wedges of land that they called 'green zones'. These wedges circle the city in an arc from the coast at Werribee to the Mornington Peninsula. The intent was to provide what was termed 'breathing space'. Other green areas, less formally designated, were set aside for future development, including freeways.

If you open a Melway street directory from the late sixties it's the creek lines that are overlaid with broken lines, signifying the possibility of development, and nowadays almost all Melbourne's freeways trace the path of a creek run underground. There are now major freeways from the CBD out to Gippsland (what used to be called the South Eastern and is now the Monash), from Collingwood to Ringwood and beyond (the Eastern). The Tullamarine Freeway now takes you well past the airport, while the Calder goes all the way to Bendigo and the Hume sends you to Albury-Wodonga. CityLink joins the Monash and takes you across the West Gate to Geelong, the Metropolitan Road joins up the Hume, the Monash and the Eastern and ... well, you get the picture. It adds up to a lot of freeway. Those long-reaching tentacles of the railway lines have resulted in a city that covers a lot of ground, and these days it takes a lot of road and petrol to get around.

Why is it that the rivers were rerouted and the

creeks sacrificed to make way for these freeways? According to Merri Creek activist Ann McGregor, they were 'the line of least resistance'. There was no need to buy up or knock down houses to allow the freeway to go through. It also solved the problem of Melbourne's pesky waterways and their tendency to flood. In 1974, serious flooding damaged swathes of residential areas and water management was becoming a political issue. Rather than discourage people from living in flood-prone areas — often some of the most beautiful spots — it was easier to concrete up the creeks. That way engineers could estimate what volumes of water a creek could accommodate, and they could have some semblance of control over the water's movement. As Bruce McGregor, husband of Ann and also a Merri Creek activist, puts it: 'Drainage engineers didn't think of creeks as natural waterways, they regarded them as drains. Moonee Moonee Chain of Ponds, well, you can see what they did to that — completely concrete-lined the waterway. And if you concrete line the waterway you can't possibly do regenerative plantings along the stream edge.'

Once the home of the Wurundjeri-willam people, and the possible site of Batman's dubious treaty with the Kulin nation on 8 June 1835,

Merri Creek has seen, in the last thirty years, the return of both wildlife and people to its banks. The McGregors and others nursed it back to health from a near death after it had been used as a dumping ground for factory pollution, dead pets and rusting old cars. When I walked along the creek in late 2009 the water was clear. There was a hawk's nest tucked up high on a power pylon, native grasses, a disused quarry, trees, birds and dozens of people out for a stroll. It's a special place, but its unexpected, gentle beauty has been hard won. It was soon after that walk that I interviewed Bruce and Ann, residents of Brunswick and key members of Friends of Merri Creek, about the work they'd done to salvage 30 kilometres of unconcreted creek. It became clear to me that the survival of this waterway, and its contribution to the quality of life of people who live in this part of Melbourne, took twenty-three years of consistent and committed community action.

Towards the end of my interview with the McGregors, Bruce digressed. In his meandering, there was, as there always is, poetry:

> In the Melbourne area we get migratory birds that are involved with four migration patterns, maybe five. One of the patterns is northern Australia

to southern Australian — these are birds like reed warblers. They nest in Victoria in the summer and they live in Queensland in the winter, they're the original grey nomads. That's been going on for millions of years. So people might go to the Merri Creek and think, oh, there's nothing here, but the reed warblers nest there in the summer half year. Then we get birds that migrate from Tasmania; several species have summer in Tasmania and then winter here. We get birds that are altitudinal migrants, so that means in summer they're in the mountains and in the winter they're down on the plains — robins, for example. And there are also birds that are erratic in their movements depending on the food, so they move around different parts of Victoria. Cockatoos and honeyeaters. As there's been a drought in country Victoria for years they've tended to hang around southern Victoria and Melbourne because there's been food, and we've been planting trees for thirty years now so they have somewhere to forage.

When Bruce spoke like that, I saw that the air above the city is full of purposeful movement. The places we think of as empty are not. They are full. And this is a place that we share.

Sometimes it's wildlife, plants, people and birds that fill Melbourne up but a place can also be thick with meaning – what Melbourne writer Maria Tumarkin calls a traumascape. It's been over thirty years since part of the West Gate Bridge fell down, but it's still not possible for someone of my age or older to drive across it and not think about what happened there. The families of some of the victims still refuse to travel on it, accessing the west through Footscray instead. Virginia and I had plenty of time to think about these things one day in early October as the traffic banked up for miles because of roadworks to increase the number of lanes on the bridge. (One hundred and sixty thoussand cars drive over the bridge each day, four times the expected capacity in 1970.) For all these reasons the disaster gets a starring role in the opening scene of Peter Temple's *Truth*:

> One spring morning in 1970, the bridge's half-
> built steel frame stood in the air, it crawled with
> men, unmarried men, men with wives, men with
> wives and children, men with children they did not
> know, men with nothing but the job and the hard,
> hard hangover and then Span 10–11 failed.

One hundred and twelve metres of newly
raised steel and concrete, two thousand tonnes.

Men and machines, tools, lunchboxes, toilets,
whole sheds — even, someone said, a small black
dog, barking — all fell down the sky. In moments,
thirty-five men were dead or dying, bodies broken,
sunk in the foul grey crusted sludge of the Yarra's
bank. Diesel fuel lay everywhere. A fire broke out
and, slowly, a filthy plume rose to mark the scene.

The building of the West Gate Bridge began in
1968. In March 1970 workers on the bridge held
a stop-work meeting because of safety concerns —
a bridge under construction in the United States
using similar engineering techniques had run into
problems. This stop-work meeting was just one in
what was ongoing action. Then, on 15 October
1970, 2000 tonnes of steel box girder grids fell
45 metres. Workers inside the hollow spans that
fell were killed, and those in the contruction huts
below were crushed. Despite miraculous stories of
men who'd 'ridden' their spans down, thirty-five
people died that day and seventeen were critically
injured. Some survivors died in years to come of
stress-related diseases. One survivor, Des Gibson,
was pulled out of the water only to have four heart

attacks in the next three years. He was dead at thirty-two.

It was one of those events that made people stop. People remember exactly where they were when it happened. The photo that led the *Sun*'s report on 16 October was taken by a ten-year-old boy, Udo Rockman, who was out on a primary school excursion. 'I took one picture of the bridge and then we heard an explosion', Udo said.

> So I put my camera up again and took another. At first I thought they were blowing something up. Then we realised the bridge was falling. I didn't see any men, but some of the other boys and girls said men were jumping and falling from it. When the bridge hit, it caught fire.

I was six years old. I didn't see the rivets 'spat from the span like bullets from a machine gun' or bodies drowned in mud or flattened so there was 2 metres between their shoulders. I would not have understood why many of the victims had to be left under the spans until the steel was cut up and removed. But I vividly remember the shock of it. My brother, who was only four at the time, tells me he does too. It was not simply the fact of the deaths or the violent nature of them but the *idea* of it: the bridge was intended as a symbol of modern Melbourne, much as the Royal Exhibition Building had been a century before. And it had failed. As an editorial in *The Age* written after the collapse said, 'The West Gate Bridge, which yesterday morning was a symbol of Melbourne's growth and enterprise, is now a monument to many dead men'.

The West Gate wasn't only intended as an example of the kind of modern engineering that cities liked to showcase. It was also meant to connect the working-class suburbs to more affluent suburbs, to link a divided city and open it out to the industrial lands in the west. But after its fall the bridge became a symbol of something else: the power of the Victorian unions at that time and the increasing attack on those unions in the years that followed.

Most of the men who died in the West Gate Bridge disaster were metal workers. After 15 October unions black banned the site. The royal commission into the collapse delivered its report in August 1971 and found that the unions' industrial campaign was one of the reasons the project was under strain. Work didn't resume on the bridge for several more months.

The commission's ruling was the beginning of the diminishment of Melbourne's union movement, helped along by the government's antagonism towards the powerful Builders Labourers Federation led by Norm Gallagher. Under Gallagher, the BLF helped preserve historic boulevards like Royal Parade from development and saved many historic buildings – such as the Regent Theatre and the City Baths – from destruction. The BLF did have a reputation for corruption, however, and Gallagher was jailed for accepting bribes in 1992, the same year that Jeff Kennett became premier of the state. That was also the year that a stonemason used a caricature of Kennett's face as inspiration for a gargoyle being carved into St Patrick's Cathedral during renovation.

When the West Gate Bridge was completed in 1978 it was years behind schedule and millions over budget. The final cost of its construction was $202 million. But it has to be said that it is an elegant and simple bridge. At its highest point, 58 metres, the views across western Melbourne's urban landscape are breathtaking, particularly so at night when the graphic industrial beauty to be found in the shipping containers is offset by dock lights and the flames that shoot up from the Altona Gasworks in a display much more effective than those flames outside Crown Casino.

In 2007 I worked in Footscray and drove along Docklands Highway every day. I became very fond of the massive colourful shipping crates that spread the length of the highway from the edge of the city to the Maribyrnong River. The offices I was heading to were in a warehouse down on that river, a warehouse with a fairly typical Footscray history. From 1906 until the Second World War the site was used by Barnet Glass Rubber. Then it became a cotton mill, and consequently one of Footscray's biggest employers during the war. Since 2000 the warehouse has been the international headquarters of the travel guide publishers, and an extraordinary Melbourne story, Lonely Planet. Tony and Maureen Wheeler put their early books together around a kitchen table before moving their growing business to offices in Hawthorn and, finally, Footscray. The name they chose for their enterprise was a charming accident, as Tony Wheeler explains:

> We had just been to see a movie called *Mad Dogs and Englishmen* ... And one of the songs in the film had a line about travelling across the sky and seeing a lonely planet. And I thought that sounded nice, but Maureen corrected me, that it didn't say

'lonely planet' at all, he was actually singing 'lovely planet.' So in a way, the name has been a mistake.

While I was working at Lonely Planet I witnessed another of those publishing endings I seem to specialise in. The Wheelers sold a large percentage of their share in the business for unnamed millions of dollars to the BBC. They then set up the Wheeler Foundation, which became the major patron of Melbourne's Centre of Books, Writing and Ideas. It became the Wheeler Centre in spring 2009.

I would often go up to the cafeteria on the roof of the mill and look east, over the docks, to the Melbourne skyline, which is picture-book perfect from that perspective. I liked to photograph it because it struck me as a kind of urbanised version of Uluru: a textured plane that turned grey when storms approached and lit up gold at sunset, that reflected the sky and clouds back at you while sea gulls circled up high in an endless vigil. It is one of my favourite views in Melbourne.

While I don't work in Footscray any more, I often go across to visit the *Overland* office or to see friends. Footscray is an industrial suburb and its pretty streets are cut through by some of the city's busiest thoroughfares such as Ballarat and Geelong roads, roads dense with trucks that thunder out west. In recent years young families have been venturing there, lured by timber cottages, Californian bungalows and big backyards. Perhaps a sign of the suburb's rise (or fall, depending on your point of view), in 2009 Melbourne's famous (and now national) St Jerome's Laneway Festival was about to move from the constriction of the CBD's Caledonian Lane and surrounds to the grounds of the Footscray Community Arts Centre.

In her survey of the suburb's gentrification, Australian-Vietnamese writer Thuy Linh Nguyen wrote:

> According to the 2009 Footscray Strategic report, more and more skilled workers, students, and university-qualified residents are settling in the area. Average household incomes are on the rise and so are real estate prices. On a grocery run, I spot a new development shadowing Little Saigon Market – a concrete monolith on the corner where the Chinese chess-players used to meet. And next to the Italian solicitors, the Ethiopian cafes, and the Vietnamese electrical repair shops, the Barkly Theatre is being converted into sixty luxury apartments.

Luxury apartments are a long way away from Footscray's beginnings as a tiny settlement around a punt on the 'Saltwater River', as the Maribyrnong River was then known. The punt provided a crossing point for travellers to Williamstown. There's still a punt today, though on a different spot, and it's mainly used by cyclists. The crossing is a gentle, eccentric little trip that gives you a sense of how wide and fast the choppy grey water gets when the Maribyrnong hits the Yarra, before opening out to the sea.

'Saltwater', as the cluster of shacks became known, grew into a suburb named after the village of Foots on the River Cray in Kent. During the second half of the 19th century it became the centre of the slaughtering industry and was home to the largest cattle yards in the Southern Hemisphere. Related trades, such as glue works, tanneries and bone mills, moved to Footscray as well. Keeping a city in food and clothes is dirty, polluting work and the Maribyrnong River ran with chemicals, blood and guts. The punt trip became pretty damn smelly and the river approach to Melbourne earnt it the appellation 'Marvellous Smelbourne'.

The abattoir in Footscray didn't close that long ago and it once employed the father of well-known cartoonist Michael Leunig and, briefly, young Leunig himself. The words 'I had to go up and start the train moving, and I'd have to kill the first dozen or so cattle with a bolt gun' sit queerly coming from such a gentle man, though perhaps they shouldn't. The site has now been turned into river parklands and returned to the wetlands from which it arose.

Waves of migrants and refugees arrived from Europe after the Second World War, and by 1966 almost one-third of Footscray's population had been born overseas. At the same time, Footscray's manufacturing industry was falling away and there was substantial unemployment. By the 1980s many recent Vietnamese migrants had moved to Footscray. The suburb, rightly or wrongly, became associated with Melbourne's heroin trade, and its train station was assumed to be the go-to place for drugs. Footscray's most recent immigrants are African and the population now comes from more than 135 different countries, speaking more than eighty-five languages. Thuy Linh Nguyen again:

> During such transition periods, Footscray is at its most diverse. Hopkins Street is a mishmash of the past and present. T. Cavallero and Sons' pasticceria continues to sell cannoli next to the Vietnamese pho shops. A few doors down, Awash Ethiopian Restaurant offers wat with injera. Over time, ailing businesses like Cheap n' Chic will make way

for halal butchers, yoghurt houses, and Pakistani grocers, while Footscray continues to serve as the new immigrant's town.

The increasing Indian population in Footscray meant that suburb was particularly affected when several Indian students were bashed in 2009. International education is Victoria's largest export industry (it's worth $4.5 billion a year) and 50 000 international students are living in Melbourne at any given time. The economic implications of potentially racially motivated crimes like this were enormous and the state government was quick to be seen to respond to the situation. If only the same keenness was shown when responding to racism where there was less of an economic imperative to sort out the problem.

If you're driving back across the West Gate, from Williamstown towards the city, you see how impressive Melbourne has become, with the sweep of the Bolte Bridge riding high above what used to be the arse end of the city. If you look north-west you see the silver CityLink sound tube that takes you down to the Tullamarine Freeway and has become the background for several luxury car ads and a music video for the band Spiderbait.

The multi-award-winning architecture firm Denton Corker Marshall designed much of this urban landscape. The firm has come a long way since City Square and was responsible for several big developments during the Kennett era. Their visual style has come to represent corporate contemporary Melbourne, and that vivid canary yellow, derided when *Vault* was unveiled, is there wherever you come across their work. John Denton, one of the firm's partners, has been the state architect since 2005. Denton Corker Marshall's projects includes the Adelphi hotel, renowned for the glass-bottomed swimming pool that hangs over Flinders Lane (and sharp-cornered metal coffee tables that have injured many a shin on many a romantic weekend); the Melbourne Museum, which sits in the Exhibition Gardens; Jeff's shed; the sinuous roads of the Tullamarine/Calder interchange and the Bolte Bridge; and the yellow and red salutes that form Melbourne Gateway along the section of the Tullamarine that ends at Flemington Road.

Soon after the freeway extension was opened, architect Anthony Styant-Browne echoed an idea that my father, Peter, raised in *The What If Man*:

architects were playing with science fiction's imagining of our future. Styant-Browne wrote:

> Weaving through the composition are ribbons of freeway, one of which leads through a glimmering, elliptical bridge tunnel called 'the sound tube'. Designed to be experienced at 100kph, the ensemble works equally well coming and going. From the north, at the Brunswick Road exit, the freeway curves to reveal the city skyline seconds before the red sticks hove into view, enfilade, connected at the top to the yellow beam forming, for an instant, a portal. Seconds later, the thin red line breaks into its constituent pieces, the beam separates (becoming a boom) and the orange slash of wall appears ... At night, the white-lit sound tube hovers above Flemington Road like a flying saucer in a B-grade 1950s sci-fi movie ... this place, this moment of pure aesthetic pleasure may be City Link's greatest gift to Melbourne.

Denton Corker Marshall's work is quite different to that of other prominent architectural firms such as ARM (Docklands, St Kilda Library) or Wood Marsh (ACCA, EastLink freeway), both of which have a more organic approach that produces less predictable solutions. Nonetheless Denton Corker

Marshall's buildings and roads have an elegance and lightness – in terms of both materials and natural light used – that offsets Melbourne's historical tendency towards weight and gloom. Their use of colour is confident, energetic and cheerful. They are unabashedly modern in their sensibility and convey the sense of a city 'going somewhere'. Which begs the question: 'Where?'

Summer, again

The Yarra has always been a social divide in Melbourne. At first this was because the rich lived south of the river and the poor lived north of it. These days the divide is more a cultural one, albeit imagined. In December, a friend who hailed from Albert Park decided to organise a picnic locally, in St Vincent's Place. Here is the ensuing email exchange:

Chris: Just a quick follow up regarding Saturday's drinks in St Vincent's Gardens. There are two very easy trams that go very close, we will be just off Montague Street. The no. 96 tram goes from Nicholson Street to Albert Park light rail station, at which point cross the tracks, walk down Bridport Street (which has shops) and turn right at Montague Street. The Park will be on your left. The No. 1 (South Melbourne) tram goes down Lygon and Swanston streets to Albert Park.

Get out at Bridport Street and backtrack half a block down Montague to the park. I should warn my North Fitzroy friends that both trams will take you OVER THE RIVER. This is meant to happen, just act normal.

Helen: I am uncertain how to prepare for this epic journey. Should we bring lifejackets?

Mike: Wait, what? Hold on – you mean if you keep heading south there's a RIVER?!

Susannah: It's all right everyone; I've found a map.

Tom: Ha! I'm all up for journeys to far-flung climes. As long as I can bring my cynical North-of-the-river sneer and sense of intellectual superiority and be sneered at in turn by those with an inflated sense of their own prettiness and of their importance to the city's arts (see television) culture.

Matt: Will there be somewhere for me to park my fixie?

Ciannon: Tom, you are most welcome to bring your intellectual superiority, because that side of town has a firmly entrenched financial superiority, which trumps anything the likes of us can supply. They do also have Andrews Hamburgers.

This social split is also essential to Christos Tsiolkas's *The Slap*. In that novel Harry, who lives in one of Melbourne's beachside suburbs, slaps a child who lives in Fitzroy, with traumatic consequences for all concerned:

> [Harry] drove across the bridge but instead of heading south down Kings Way he turned north and drove through the city. He kept driving and turned into Brunswick Street. The traffic was heavier and there were people everywhere. He kept driving north and he found himself weaving across the small streets of Fitzroy. He found the street. He parked the car and sat in the darkness, looking at the house. Even in the dark the house looked ramshackle, uncared for. The grass hadn't been mown for months, their kid could get lost in it. He took a deep breath. The creek and the river were close by — weren't they scared of rats, mice, tiger snakes for God's sake? ... There was nothing for him to do. The future would exact his revenge.
>
> He drove. He drove south, heading towards the water, heading towards home ...
>
> The car seemed to fly down Hotham Street and then he turned and could see glimmering lights on the dark water of the bay.

I ventured across that divide to live in St Kilda East, or Balaclava, as parts of it are called, for a couple of years. I needed that distinctive light and sense of openness you get in seaside suburbs, that faint whiff of salt. Balaclava is given distinction by its large Orthodox Jewish community, which, for non-believers like me, meant greater access to bagels, lox and kugelhopf. Its Safeway also had the craziest car park in Melbourne (rivalled, perhaps, by that of Piedimonte's supermarket in North Fitzroy), and I often thought I should make a short film, using time-lapse photography, of the shenanigans that took place in the car park next to Wall 280 cafe.

There were a few months when Virginia and I lived together in that flat, and she'd ride to her job at the Melbourne Museum in Carlton. That meant cycling down St Kilda Road and through the city. She was, as many cyclists are, car-doored a couple of times – that is, had a driver open their door into her path, causing her to crash – and she'd been severely bruised. Despite these kinds of dangers Melbourne is a great place to ride, not least because it's flat. Since the first penny-farthing arrived in Melbourne in 1875 (similar, really, to the now popular fixie), our citizens have been keen on their bikes. One hundred and twenty years ago, penny-farthing races were held at the Exhibition Gardens and the MCG. In 1909 Snowy Munro clocked 7 hours 12 minutes 51 seconds in the Warrnambool to Melbourne Classic, beating the steam train by five minutes. A century ago Melbourne hosted the world's first bicycle wedding.

After those enthusiastic beginnings, cycling tailed off in the middle of the last century as the car took off. But as petrol prices rise and traffic jams get worse, the enthusiasm has returned. This means, of course, that now the roads are full of *both* cyclists and cars. And, as the number of riders increase, drivers are becoming increasingly irritated at having to take cyclists into account. Critical Mass, a worldwide collective dedicated to making cities around the world more bike friendly, has been organising monthly bike rides through Melbourne's CBD since 1995 in an attempt to assert cyclists' right to share the road. They've also ridden in Burnley Tunnel and on CityLink in protest at those freeways' lack of bike lanes. Depending on your point of view, Critical Mass participants are environmentally friendly or rabid – and rapid – political activists. The level of rage directed at riders can't just be about the fact that some drivers have been frightened by cyclists' unpredictability.

The idea of cycling-friendly cities has become the stuff of ideological battle: in short, if you denounce cars you're denouncing capitalism. You're also a smug bastard.

This was the context in which, at the end of September 2009, much-loved performer Magda Szubanski launched into a routine about cyclists on television show *Good News Week*, ultimately exhorting viewers to open their car doors as cyclists rode past. Her anger and humour was directed at a group of cyclists who ride down the beach road to Black Rock and back most mornings around dawn, at pretty ferocious speeds. Certainly, it's true that people have died. In 2008 an elderly pedestrian was killed at a crossing by a cyclist who failed to stop. But cyclists are dying as well. In 2008 a tourist bus hit a 33-year old woman riding down Swanston Street. Overall 280 riders sustained serious injuries and five cyclists died due to collisions with vehicles on Victorian roads in 2008. For all these reasons I couldn't laugh, and I was relieved when, a few days later, Szubanski made a public apology.

It felt like quite an epic journey when, on the first weekend of December, I rode my bike to St Kilda to watch Sian Prior do a reading at the local library. To get there I pedalled down that grand tree-lined boulevard St Kilda Road, crossing the great divide. Just over the Princes Bridge I passed the geometric monoliths of the Victorian Arts Centre and the NGV – where *Weeping Woman* was snatched. There have been arguments about whether the buildings in the arts precinct live up to the original design of modernist architect Roy Grounds, but there's no doubt that the NGV, the first building to be built, does. The gallery is a bluestone rectangle surrounded by a moat with a wall of water at the entrance. There is something profoundly Melbourne about the building, which takes the local bluestone – a stone that the Old Melbourne Jail and Pentridge Prison make look so deadly – and gives it a sheer splendour by allowing water to surround it, to run over it, to create splashes of dark illumination much as you get when a river rapid runs over boulders. As a child the wall of water entranced me more than the art and when I visit the gallery there are always children who, as I did, are holding their hands to the glass, watching the water make way for them.

The St Kilda Library is a more unassuming but equally impressive building. Designed by ARM, its curved, pale stone facade extends the sense of light and the waves of the beachside suburb. At the same time the facade resembles the page of a book. There were twenty or so people there to watch Sian read from her *Meanjin* essay on the Balibo Five and East Timor. The Timorese independence movement has always had a strong support base in Melbourne because one of the two news teams that were murdered at Balibo in 1975 had come from Melbourne (HSV-7). The youngest man to die, 21-year-old Tony Stewart, had a young brother himself. Paulie Stewart went on to sing in the band Painters and Dockers and has been an advocate for East Timor in the thirty-five years since his brother's death. After the reading we headed off for a beer at the Local Taphouse, which has around twenty boutique beers on tap. These days Melbourne has more micro-breweries and beer bars than you can poke a bottle of chardonnay at.

St Kilda was on the agenda again a couple of weeks later, during the inevitable 'what will we do this New Year's Eve?' conversations. We'd been asked to a party in St Kilda but that seemed too far to ride on a hot night. The mid-thirties temperatures were, however, an improvement on New Year's Eve two years earlier, when it had still been 40 degrees at midnight (though I have to say that nude Scrabble-playing with cold beer is one of my fonder New Year's memories). Driving was out of the question if we wanted to drink, and taxis are impossible to get on New Year's Eve.

So, there was no river crossing. This year, fully clothed, and with beer in our backpacks, we cycled along the Canning Street bike path and then along the Park Street path into Brunswick and to a barbecue at a friend's. At about 9 pm the wind picked up and streaks of lightening zig-zagged across the sky. Twenty of us stood, like a group of kids, watching. When the rain finally hit, it was torrential and we all got overexcited. We – the youngest of us being about twenty-six and the oldest, me, being forty-six – played a game in which we ran under the grapevine, past the Hills hoist, down the long length of the quarter-acre block and touched the back fence. The rain was so thick that this pretty simple manoeuvre was quite difficult. Those who were reluctant to get soaked were clapped, loudly, until they did the bolt. Apparently the city fireworks almost didn't go ahead because of the rain, but they did in the end and we stood in the street and watched the reflections of the fireworks on the clouds. At midnight there was more than the usual amount of kissing – all that clean air, I suppose – then Virginia and I got on our bikes in the pouring rain and rolled down the slight incline that stretches between Brunswick and Fitzroy feeling like it was the best New Year's Eve in a long time. Rain: it could only mean good things.

The next night there was more rain and more barbecue. This time we went to Stuart Geddes' house. He and his partner, Penny, lived at the end of a lane off Easey Street in Collingwood, just behind the Robert Burns pub, and it was nice to have a new association with a street forever haunted for me by Suzanne Armstrong and Susan Bartlett: their youthful faces, their beautiful smiles and their pretty seventies summer dresses.

The old fence that divided Stuart and Penny's house from the cafe next door was weighed down with so much morning glory that it took up half the yard. We sat outdoors surrounded by the feral vine, watching the most extraordinary purple-pink sunset reveal itself in flashes as dense black clouds raced overhead. The claps of thunder were so close we wondered if we were about to be struck. We retreated to the concrete outdoor area under the leaking corrugated iron roof and started up a game of mahjong. Penny taught us how to shuffle the tiles, build the wall, and chow and pung and kong. Dad had played the game with my brother and me when we were kids, using a set made of bone and bamboo, but that was long ago. These tiles were plastic and the rules a distant memory, but the twittering of the birds (as the shuffling is called) still had real resonance, beckoning me back to childhood.

The new year was underway. The green buds of the leaves on the Cape Lilac pushed through the clusters of beads. The baubles fell to the ground, where they lay, in ever-increasing piles, until we found the time to shovel huge quantities of them into the bin. The pretty lilac flowers that came out soon after were only slightly mollifying. The state government decided to 'do something' about the violence that seemed to engulf the CBD's King Street — a strip of the city lined with 24-hour drinking venues — most Saturday nights. Police enacted new search laws in which they could declare areas designated search zones if they have a history of weapon use: Footscray was the test suburb. The hot north-westerlies were whipping across Hoddle's grid, much as the grid funnels cold south-westerly winds up from the sea in winter. Minister for Transport Lynne Kosky resigned, not, as was assumed, because Melbourne's introduction of a new ticketing scheme for public transport was now running extremely late and over budget, but for personal reasons. Sam the Koala – who became famous in the wake of Black Saturday for the touching photo of her accepting water from a fireman – became a feature exhibit in the foyer of the Melbourne Museum. She'd been euthanised a few months earlier because she suffered the unglamorous condition of chlamydia and was being remembered for 'her extraordinary role in providing a source of hope to those devastated by the February bushfires'. I was appalled that she was to be stuffed and permanently on display, but hard pressed to articulate why this seemed so wrong.

On Australia Day we were back at Stuart and Penny's for another barbecue. The morning glory had by now dragged the fence over so their back-yard appeared to bleed into the cafe next door. This time we were there to celebrate our friend Jeremy Wortsman's citizenship ceremony over snags and pavlova. Born and bred in Brooklyn, Jeremy had chosen Melbourne as his town for much the same reason I had: he liked the people here.

Back in late October 2009 the Yarra City council (an amalgam of what had been the Fitzroy, Richmond, Collingwood and Carlton councils) had announced that it had 'resolved to introduce Local Law No.8, which will empower police to request that people drinking in unlicensed areas on the streets of Yarra at any time of the day pour out opened drinks'. I didn't really understand the implications of this until Virginia returned home from boot camp – now held in Fitzroy Gardens due to yet another dreary by-law – to report that Fitzroy's homeless, pushed down to Smith Street by gentrification, had been pushed out of the suburb altogether and were fighting the Fitzroy Gardens parkies for space to sleep undercover. (Fitzroy Gardens are actually in the city and fall under Melbourne City Council's pervue.)

It was one of many changes being made to the liquor laws. From 1 January 2010 pubs were automatically classified as 'high risk' if they were open until 3 am. This affected most of Melbourne's live music venues as well as the barn-like drinking venues that the high-risk category was directed at. The costs associated with being designated 'high risk' – increased licence fees and the hiring of at least two security guards every night of the week – pushed running costs of music venues up by as much as five times. Frustration over the situation finally erupted when one of the grottiest of them, the Tote, in Collingwood, announced it would have to close.

Writer and broadcaster Marieke Hardy was just one of hundreds of people who were appalled. Her description (published on ABC's *The Drum* website) of the pub was vivid, to say the least:

> The Tote hotel was never the prettiest of venues
> – in fact for the most part it was a stinking,
> sweaty bitch mistress, luring blinking punters in
> off Johnston Street with the promise of grubby
> sex in the toilets and twelve-minute guitar solos,
> and propelling them back out into the night with
> bleeding ear drums and the sort of blossoming
> liver problems once enjoyed by a young and
> wild-eyed Oliver Reed ... And now it has been
> dragged to its death by tepid bureaucracy and
> a few rather dull scuffles over money. Nobody
> ever pulled out knives at the Tote, nobody pawed
> intrusively at passing women ... Young men will
> continue to be knocked down to their deaths on
> cigarette-stained footpaths outside lairy nightclubs

and one by one the damp, dark, unassuming live music venues where the most violent acts play out onstage between consenting adults will be quietly packed away and left behind. And eventually, state governments will no longer be able to swing their dicks around about which city has the most thriving arts scene, because there will no longer be any.

Melbourne has always been enthusiastic about music. In 1967 a staggering 200 000 people – close to 10 per cent of the city's population at the time – turned up at the Myer Music Bowl to hear the Seekers play. They were one of Melbourne's first bands to become truly internationally famous. Audiences like this encouraged a strong rock independent music scene that, in the early seventies, included bands such as Daddy Cool and Skyhooks.

As a teenager, and for reasons that now seem nonsensical, I had to choose between Sherbet and Skyhooks. I chose Skyhooks (I do believe history has validated that great life decision). Two high school friends, Greg Macainsh and Fred Strauks, started the band in 1973. They found their lead singer, Graeme 'Shirley' Strachan, at the Village Green Hotel in Mount Waverley watching Max Merritt and the Meteors one Sunday afternoon.

Macainsh described the times thus:

> It's 1972, and I'm at Swinburne Film and
> Television College trying to persuade myself
> that it might be like the art schools that British
> musicians went to ... I'm restless and writing
> songs with more intent than ever. A Trotskyite
> cook by the name of Steve Hill ... enters my
> radar ... Steve finds Redmond Symons in the
> Carlton band Scumbag and appeals to his latent
> opportunism. We've got gigs and a roadie with a
> van. Scumbag doesn't, so Red brings his Les Paul,
> silk pants, black gumboots and brattish intellect
> to the fold.

I'd picked Team Skyhooks in part because they had the names of actual Melbourne places in songs such as 'Lygon Street Limbo' and 'Balwyn Calling', though Macainsh's lyrics to 'All My Friends are Getting Married' rang more true for me in early 2010, when I had a wedding every weekend, than they did in the mid-seventies. Adulthood had also helped me put a name to the excitement I felt back in 1976 when I saw AC/DC's Bon Scott, in his extraordinarily tight pants, singing 'It's a Long Way to the Top (If You Wanna Rock 'n' Roll)' while standing in the back of a truck being driven down the tram tracks in Swanston Street, accompanied by bagpipers – the scene complete with the since demolished Gas and Fuel buildings in the background. And yes, while some of that excitement was about sex, it was also about trams, and Swanston Street, and seeing my city full of sexually charged energy screened on television at 6 pm on Sunday night on the government-owned ABC.

It didn't seem strange to me that Skyhooks or AC/DC had members from my hometown, or that the television show that, musically anyway, defined my generation was another local production. On re-reading Peter Wilmoth's *Glad All Over*, I found this wonderful quote from musician Paul Hester – may he rest in peace – that demonstrates just how deep into Melbourne's culture *Countdown* went:

> I was in make-up one day and Winsome McCaughey was there to be on the *7.30 Report*. I was in a bit of a cocky mood, so I went up to her and said, 'Winsome McCaughey? Paul Hester of Crowded House. It's about these parking fines, Winsome. Whaddya reckon, you could pull a few strings down at the old Town Hall?' She got me back. She stood there and decided to get dressed for the show right there and then. She pulled her dress up over her head and pulled her tights

over undies. We sort of sat there and said, 'Holy Christ, that's the Lord Mayor!' She didn't bat an eyelid.

Melbourne, like many places, experienced the punk explosion from 1977 onwards – meaning punk was born about the same time as community radio station Triple R. Music historian Clinton Walker recalls those days:

> I remember vividly those Tuesday nights at the Tiger Lounge in Richmond in the winter of 1978 … I remember gigs at the tiny Exford Hotel in Russell Street, at Melbourne University and other places – the legendary Crystal Ballroom came later … I'd come all the way from Brisbane to be part of it.

The most famous band of this era was the Birthday Party, led by Nick Cave. Mick Harvey, a member of that band, draws a direct line between Melbourne's embrace of the suburbs and the development of punk. There was a comfort in the suburbs that he, and others, found stifling creatively: 'By the time I reached my late teens I was happy to drift to the inner city'.

In the nineties Melbourne boasted, among others, Frente, the Meanies, Even, Icecream Hands

and Magic Dirt (via Geelong). The decade also her-
alded the coming of hip-hop, a scene supported by
Melbourne's vibrant graffiti culture. Here's DJ and
Triple R announcer Declan Kelly on the subject:

> Music for music fiends, the eternal beat diggers
> mentality of hip-hop served to introduce crowds
> to the sounds of funk, soul, disco, electro, boogie,
> rock and other strains of music that hip-hop
> sampled. Clubs such as Razor, Purveyors and
> Cocoa Butter led the way until the house, jungle
> and rave scenes bloomed in the early nineties.
> By the end of the [nineties] Melbourne was a
> key stop for techno, drum and bass and house
> pioneers from around the world.

In 2000 Melbourne group the Avalanches released
their distinctive, influential and life-affirming
album *Since I Left You*. It contained extracts from
600 different records (by artists including Donny
Osmond, Kid Creole & the Coconuts, Madonna
and Boney M) and hundreds of individual samples,
including everything from golf instructionals to a
horse neighing. It took two years to record in Richmond's Sing Sing studios and almost as long again
for copyright clearances to go through.

Melbourne's music scene was the result of both

the number of independently owned pubs and the support it received from Triple R. The station has been going since late 1976 and has the largest number of subscribers (per capita) of any public radio station in the world. Half its budget is raised from subscriptions every year, and the announcers all provide their services for free. (Well, except for the Breakfasters – people don't tend to volunteer to get up at 5 am five days a week.) During the late 1970s and early 1980s Triple R was synonymous with the alternative music scene. Like punk, the station often got itself into trouble. As *Age* journalist Larissa Dubecki wrote:

> Its litany of troublemaking, detailed in Mark
> Phillips' unofficial biography of the station
> *Radio City*, is long and varied but never boring. It
> immortalises volunteer John Kleiman as one of the
> first to feel the wrath of the conservative Australian
> Broadcasting Tribunal after playing a piece in which
> American comedian Richard Pryor used the word
> 'motherf—ker' and described rubbing cocaine on
> his penis to stimulate his sex drive. (Kleiman was
> sacked and RRR's licence was reduced from three
> years to one by an irate broadcasting tribunal.)

There are no set playlists and no formal radio

voices. Individual hosts play whatever they like, leading to a real variety and depth of music. Triple R was the first radio station to mix sport and intellectual play, in a style that is unique to Melbourne. The station is not dependent on government funding or ratings so political chat isn't compromised – it's encouraged. There isn't another radio station like it in Australia.

Triple R was almost closed on several occasions. Like the pubs that are the backbone of the city's live music scene, the station has had to fight time and time again to survive. Declan Kelly notes:

> The live scene showed stoic resistance with campaigns such as Fair Go 4 Live Music, launched when institutions such as the Empress and Bar Open in Fitzroy and the Town Hall Hotel in North Melbourne were threatened in 2003. Melbourne bucked the revolt against live music, staving off the residents, developers and poker machines that quashed band venues in other Australian cities.

Melbourne enjoys its cool bars and laneways and cosmopolitan drinking culture. It's easy to forget that until as recently as 1966 if Victorians wanted a drink after 6 pm they had to go to an

Italian cafe and drink it, illegally, out of a coffee mug. (No wonder Melbourne is so keen on its Italian heritage.) The end of six o'clock closing did not transform Melbourne's drinking culture. It was Victoria's *Liquor Control Act 1987*, enacted by the Cain government, that did that. That law had been passed, despite much toing and froing, after the report and recommendations by Dr John Nieuwenhuysen. He suggested the government explore ways of managing alcohol abuse other than overregulating the industry. He called for sweeping changes to laws that had been only a step up from the six o'clock swill, laws that had allowed a group of hoteliers to have a stranglehold on drinking – and the profits thereof – in the state. As Michael Harden wrote in an article for *Meanjin*, 'Every time you face the luxury of abundant choice whenever you feel like going out to dinner, you have the Nieuwenhuysen report of March 1986 to thank for it'. In 1986, there were 571 on-premises (restaurant) licences in the state; in 2004 (the most recent figures available from the Australian Bureau of Statistics) there were 5136. Harden again:

> The circumstances which brought about
> Melbourne's unique and often idiosyncratic take
> on drinking and eating were highly particular.

It would be difficult if not impossible to repeat them, which, in an ideal world, would see responses to problems take on a more imaginative cast than the clumsy one-size-fits-all approach of recent times.

In 2007 New South Wales finally modified its laws in the hope that smaller venues and bars might flourish as they do in Melbourne. The president of the NSW branch of the Australian Hotels Association, John Thorpe, was unimpressed: 'We aren't barbarians, but we don't want to sit in a hole and drink chardonnay and read a book'. Perhaps what seemed like a backhander at Melbourne and its arty pretensions was really, once again, a panicked plea to allow a relatively few large hotels to rake in profits.

In late February American singer Amanda Palmer was in town, and she was staying with Peter in Surrey Hills. We took her to our favourite pizza spot, Gertrude Street's Ladro, to meet Paul Kelly, and the two of them spent much of the evening talking about the SLAM (Save Live Australia's Music) rally that would be happening a few days later in response to the closure of the Tote.

On the day of the rally, Amanda, Paul and thousands of others met at the State Library of

Victoria. It was mid-week and during the day so I couldn't make it, but feeling about the new liquor laws was running so high that *The Age* described the rally as the largest gathering on an arts issue – though the size of that gathering was described as being anything from 10 000 to 70 000. A band was set up on the back of a flatbed truck to lead the procession along Swanston Street and up Bourke Street to Parliament House. They played, predictably, 'It's a Long Way to the Top'. Some of the bagpipers on the truck had played along to the song in the original clip some thirty-four years before. It was a moment of kitsch that some – including me – loved, and others thought was backward looking.

Speakers on the steps of Parliament House included local musicians Missy Higgins, Clare Bowditch, Tim Rogers and Evelyn Morris. Paul addressed the crowd in his tentative but charismatic fashion:

> I came to Melbourne in 1977 and started playing
> in small pubs in the inner city. Hearts, Martinis,
> the Kingston Hotel, out the back of Cafe Paradiso
> … You don't learn how to write a song at school,
> you don't do a TAFE course in how to play
> in front of an audience. These places were my
> universities.

Paul then introduced Rick Dempster of the Brunswick Blues Shooters. The band's long-running residency at North Fitzroy's Railway Hotel was one of the first victims of the liquor licensing laws. Dempster described it as a 'family hotel run by an Italian family called the Nigrellis ... They've got a big grape vine out the back you can go and sit under ... They had a cat that was always asleep next to the band,' before moving on to his larger point: 'The small venue is the centre of community cohesion'.

SLAM made a real impact. By the middle of 2010 the Tote had opened again for business (under new owners). By this stage SLAM organisers and representatives from Fair Go 4 Live Music and Music Victoria had been in discussions with the new Liquor Licensing commissioner, Mark Brennan, for some months. In October 2010 the link between live music and high-risk venues was removed altogether.

My year charting Melbourne life ended much as it had begun. With a wedding. The night that James and May got married, after a courtship involving fifteen years and two children, it was close to 40 degrees even though, generally speaking, this summer had been milder than the last. We were at the Boulevard Restaurant in Kew and people I'd known for twenty, thirty years were there. I talked to *Age* journalist Martin Flanagan about the Melbourne Football Club's latest recruit, Liam Jurrah, an initiated Walpiri man; I talked to Peter Wilmoth, another journalist, about the autobiography of footballer Ben Cousins that he was ghostwriting (an intensely complicated project that would, in the end, be completed by Malcolm Knox). The thrice-married Helen Garner gave an amusingly rueful speech on what you need to do to *stay* married; James and May's daughter Lola (who left our house when she was 108 centimetres high and nine years old, according to the pencil marks on the wall) knocked us all for six with a beautiful rendition of Carla Bruni's 'Quelqu'un m'a dit'. Dale Langley, shy, fragile and light as a tiny bird, stood beside her husband Jon, played her ukulele and sang – seven months later breast cancer would claim her life. Paul and Sian danced sweetly to Frank Sinatra's 'Fly Me to the Moon', and filmmaker Tony Ayres reminded people of sharehouses in St Kilda and Fitzroy. We all laughed when he talked of times that seemed to involve an inordinate amount of nudity and running under sprinklers.

Sprinklers. Now there was pause for thought. I remembered what Paul had written in *How to Make Gravy*:

> Once, at the bottom of a southern land, there was a city famous for its rain. It spread itself west and south around a large bay and eastwards to wooded fertile ranges and green valleys. The weather usually came from the west, off the Southern Ocean. Its winters were cold, its skies often grey and many were the days of drizzle and rain … All throughout the leafy eastern suburbs during summer, sprinklers played freely on the lawns. Hydrangeas, roses, lilies and all manner of thirsty flowers bloomed in verdant gardens. On weekends husbands luxuriously washed their cars, idly chatting to the neighbours, streaming hose in hand, as water cascaded carelessly to the street.

> All that was a long time ago.

This lush image of excess seemed as exotic, as decadent, as dated, as *Mad Men*'s Don Draper drinking whiskey for breakfast. The water at that time had, I suppose, run down concrete driveways into concrete gutters, and from there into creeks that have been turned into drains that now run into the Yarra or into the sea.

The richness, the fullness, of this place we call Melbourne — be it the bits filled with humans, history, buildings, animals or plants — was impressed on me even further during another conversation I had that night, with my dear friend Dianna Wells. She's a graphic designer but what was most engaging her was the masters in photography she was doing and her project of photographing Melbourne's liminal places: those in-between spaces that aren't city, suburb or country; spaces littered with the detritus of various attempts at expansion. Abandoned railway lines. Windswept former paddocks. That conversation became, as was often the case in my life at that time, a *Meanjin* article. She wrote:

> When I drive out of Melbourne I am always looking for the 'edge', the moment of change from urban to country: what does it look like? Because of the expansion of the urban growth boundary, centuries of history are about to be disturbed and possibly changed forever. These farms sit on the Victorian Volcanic Plain, a region for which significant urban growth and development are planned over the coming years.

Large gum trees and indigenous grasses hug
the sides of creeks – the last sign of remnant
landscapes before European settlement …
The northern side of the road is marked by a
billboard with a *sold* sticker: 'huge Victorian land
sub division – one of the last land subdivisional
opportunities in this fast growing northern
corridor'. The abandoned houses and farm
buildings I've been driving past are ruins waiting
to be pulled down. The buildings have passed
their use-by date even though some look less than
fifty years old. They lie in wait, boarded up, ready
for the bulldozers to arrive. I am reminded of the
eighteenth-century Italian artist of ruins Piranesi,
who said that 'ruins are a sign of life and not
death'.

Melbourne is surrounded by these hybrid
spaces, as well as a more clearly defined green belt
comprised of forests, grasslands and wetlands: the
lungs of Melbourne. According to the Victorian
National Parks Association, 'Development of this
area without appropriate corridors and natural
areas will prevent such movements and isolate
remaining habitat patches, leaving populations
prone to genetic inbreeding and greater risk of
extinction through local disturbances'. Officially

known as the Urban Growth Boundary, the green wedge was in the news at the time Di and I were talking because both the Brumby Labor government and the Opposition had called for a halt to the plan for a 'green wedge land grab' – that is, the rezoning of some green wedges to allow for more conventional urban development. Six months later though, the land had, indeed, been grabbed. In June 2010 the government proposed a move to amend the urban growth boundary and to remove 43 600 hectares of green wedge land for urban development. That included areas of western basalt plains, grassy woodland in the Merri and Darebin Creek catchments and the market gardens of the southeast food bowl – gardens that are also the habitat of the southern brown bandicoot.

We know where Melbourne started: it was a settlement of 177 Europeans scattered along the Yarra, the Werribee and the Moorabool rivers. By 2030 the population will be 5 million and the city will cover some 10 000 square kilometres. The question we need to ask then, is, where will Melbourne end? In 2002 Michael Buxton, then chairman of the premier's Green Wedge Taskforce, wrote:

The most viable cities in this century will be
those with the best quality environments. Our
relationship with our rural hinterland is critical
to the survival of Melbourne as a viable place to
live. If we retain this relationship, we will continue
to enjoy the vineyards of the Yarra Valley, the
beautiful landscapes of the Mornington Peninsula
and the Keilor Plains, our river valleys and the
forested hills of the Dandenongs and St Andrews.
Lose it and our city becomes just another casualty
to anonymous global urban sprawl, another city
that has obliterated the last vestiges of nature …
Melbourne has alternative futures. The future
without a green belt can be found in greater Los
Angeles and the other vast urban conglomerations
of the United States. The future with green
belts can be found in the English countryside
on the fringes of London, or on the edges of
Copenhagen or Portland, Oregon.

The population's insatiable desire for larger
houses and yards is cutting into the possibilities
for public green space. As well, the exponential
increase in real estate prices means that the government no longer buys properties that are up for sale
in an effort to create new public spaces – they are

reliant on spaces that have not yet been developed. Even if the desire is there (and that is arguable) the budget is not.

Liveable cities don't happen by accident, and their vitality is the result of small things writ large: a long trek from Healesville, a grotty laneway revived, waterbirds provided with a home in the midst of concrete. There are the campaigns, also, such as the one that saved Queen Victoria Market and Fitzroy forty years ago, those that have fought to keep our historic buildings alive and our favourite pubs going.

If reading Melbourne's history, talking to its citizens and writing a book that hopes to capture a slice of its life has taught me one thing it is this: if a city's going to be worth living in, you have to fight for it.

Afterword

My year in Melbourne's life has finished, and the book, this book, is officially closed for business. Where to end? We could go back to Windsor, where my family's story began, and walk along Chapel Street to Paterson's Cakes, one of the oldest cake shops in Melbourne. (Yes, Louisa Humphries, cakes that were bought.) Started by a Swiss pastry chef in 1916, it was open for ninety-four years. Over those decades, the southern end of Chapel Street has careened up and down market but either way my mother, grandmother and my great-grand-mother bought cakes there: sponges, eclairs, vanilla slices and Melba cake. As a child I didn't understand the reverence with which the shop was treated. It seemed a bit old-fashioned to me, with its staff in white uniforms and hats. I thought it smelt weird. I suppose the fact that people like me didn't continue their family's tradition of buying there explains why, by 2010, Paterson's was making a twentieth of the number of cakes it had been making in 1970. By mid-2010 the owner, Peter Schneider, decided to close the business. The news triggered phone calls to the shop bemoaning the loss of a store that had become an institution but Schneider, publicly anyway, refused to be sentimental. 'Melbourne's full of institutions that aren't there any more', he said. 'The list is as long as my arm.'

He's right, things are always changing. I can count on both hands what's changed since I began writing this book: Newtown S.C. has new owners; our much-loved bat tree has been cut down; Coburg's Pentridge Prison built in 1851, final resting place of Ned Kelly and the site of Australia's last legal hanging, now hosts wedding parties and has been developed into a shopping and apartment complex; Geelong has lost Gary Ablett Jr, Bomber Thompson and their dominance over the AFL; the last twenty-six W-class trams are being pulled from duty; Cathy, who moved to Melbourne just before Black Saturday has returned to NSW; dams have filled and Melbourne's water storage is back above 50 per cent; *Hey Hey it's Saturday* has been – for the last time? – removed from the television schedule; the Dimmeys redevelopment plans have been knocked back; the site of Victoria's first settlement, Sullivan Bay, has been subdivided and the allotments sold off for millions; and the Wheeler Centre, under Chrissy Sharp and Michael Williams' direction, has taken off.

Some things change, some things stay the same. As I worked on the final edit of this book the Melbourne Theatre Company presented the world premiere of David Williamson's sequel to *Don's Party*, the play that was first performed at the APG in 1969. It was called, somewhat depressingly, *Don Parties On*. Alison Croggon captured the repetitive momentum of the occasion:

> we hear, again, that Williamson is our best-selling
> playwright, a 'national myth-maker' who takes
> the pulse of our times and touches the receptive
> hearts of the masses. We hear that 'the critics'
> are unkind and out of touch with ordinary folk,
> and that the only reason people dislike his plays
> is because he's too popular … Various right wing
> pundits weigh in to opine about Williamson's
> leftiness. Various left wing pundits complain
> about his lack of leftiness. Someone (often it's
> me) says something plaintive about art. And
> everyone, his or her expectations satisfyingly met,
> has a marvellous time. Lather, rinse and repeat.

While Melbourne's relatively measured approach to development has given it character, without change the city would stagnate as it has for periods in the past. The balance between the conservative and the mercurial, and between focused activism and smart policy development, will dictate whether we still want to live here in twenty years time. Well, that, and Melbourne's old nemesis, the weather.

It was the Saturday morning of Victoria's Labour Day long weekend in early March 2010. It's a weekend on which, among other things, the achievements of those stonemasons at Fitzroy's Belvedere hotel are (distantly) remembered – mainly through a wider than usual range of sporting events. It's also the weekend of the Moomba celebrations that have been going since 1954 – the Moomba parade was a great favourite of mine when I was a child.

Me, I was celebrating by buying a new bike. I wanted a speedy commuter one, the kind with thin tires that mean you have to be really careful when you're crossing wet tram tracks. The kind that gets you where you're going fast. There are three bike shops in walking distance from my house, and I walked to them all. No, I didn't want to spend $3000; no, I didn't want a bike with a ye olde style basket that I could fill full of flowers as I rode around in a floaty print dress; and no, I didn't want (am too old for) a gearless, brakeless hipster bike, the like of which are filling Fitzroy's streets. And then I saw it: a gorgeous mint-green Bianchi, stunningly reduced in a floor stock sale. I made it mine.

Two hours later I was getting ready to ride my new bike to Triple R. For the last few months I had been a regular guest on *Aural Text*, a show about writing and the spoken word that was started by Alicia Sometimes and her partner Steve Grimwade back in 2000. Since Steve had been appointed director of the Melbourne Writers Festival, Jeff Sparrow had taken his place as the show's co-host. Jeff was hosting the show on his own for a few weeks and I was helping out, so I headed to Brunswick for some studio rehearsal time.

'Isn't there a storm coming?' asked Virginia, as I put on my helmet.

'Hours away', I replied. 'If the rain hits at all.' What I meant was that those crazy days of changeable Melbourne were over. Sometimes I missed them, sometimes I didn't.

A big blue sunny sky was doming over the northern suburbs and I pedalled into it: down the Canning Street bike path, through the back streets of Brunswick to the far end of Nicholson Street where Triple R is based (not far from that other Brunswick hippie paradise, the environmental park CERES). In the dark of the studio, Jeff and I practised our not-so-spontaneous-or-entertaining banter and chose some music. At one point it sounded like there was rain on the roof. 'I thought this place was soundproofed', I said. 'Must be heavy rain.' We shrugged, and went on with what we were doing. After I'd been there for about an hour I left.

I stepped through Triple R's heavy doors and onto Nicholson Street. There were dense, dark, grey clouds overhead and the gutters at my feet were gushing with water. The temperature had dropped ten or so degrees. So, Virginia was right, it had been about to rain. In fact, it was starting up again and it was pretty heavy. I walked into Blyth Street, where my bike was locked up and noticed that there were tree branches over the road. Not just rain, then – a storm.

In fact, while I'd been hidden away, close to March's entire average rainfall had dumped itself on the city in less than an hour, most of it as large hailstones. The drought, it seemed, had broken. Electricity was down across Melbourne and the NAB Cup semi-final — it takes place in the build-up to the AFL season — was delayed for twenty minutes as safety checks on Etihad Stadium were carried out. The races at Flemington were cancelled as rain gushed down the grandstand stairs, heavy as a waterfall. Twenty people at Moomba had to be treated for bruising caused by hail.

I rode home, fighting massive wind gusts. There was a wildness in the air; it was clean, thick and new. When I staggered in the front door of our house, freezing and soaked to the skin, the cats were still cowering under chairs and Virginia was watching footage of the flash floods in Elizabeth Street, complete with stranded trams, white water rapids you could raft on and a flooded Southern Cross Station. No horses had been swept away, but a couple of Range Rovers looked in trouble. She described to me the build-up of clouds, the sudden darkness — as if an eclipse had taken place. For no particular reason we began to laugh. I flung my wet clothes on the floor and wrapped myself in a towel to dry off. We stood together, looking out into our courtyard where hailstones still lay thick on the ground. White as snow, scattered with green leaves blown off in the storm. It was beautiful. That's it, Melbourne, I thought to myself. Show us what you're made of.

Bibliography

'Australia: Omerta in the Antipodes', *Time*, 31 January 1964.

Editorial, *Age*, 19 October 1970.

Annear, Robyn, *Bearbrass*, Black Inc., Melbourne, 2005.
Permission to quote courtesy of the publisher and the author.

Bailey, John, 'Bright star', *Age*, 25 April 2010.

Blundell, Graeme, 'The crown prince of suburbia', *Australian*,
7 February 2009; *The Naked Truth*, Hachette, Sydney, 2009.
Permission to quote courtesy of Hachette and the author.

Bottom, Bob, 'Market Murders', *George Negus Tonight*, broadcast
ABC TV, 30 August 2004.

Boyd, Robin, *The Australian Ugliness*, Text Publishing, Melbourne,
2010.

Brundett, Ross, 'The day the sky fell', *Herald Sun*, 21 May 1998.

Button, James, 'Graphic designers who challenged the norm',
Age, 10 November 2002; 'Eulogy: John Button 1933–2008',
Monthly, May 2008. Permission to quote courtesy of the
author.

Buxton, Michael, 'Melbourne's choice: green belt or urban
sprawl', *Age*, 1 October 2002. Permission to quote courtesy
of the author.

Byrnes, Paul, 'Animal Kingdom', *Sydney Morning Herald*, 5 June 2010.

Cazaly, Ciannon, 'Off the Ball: Football's History Wars', *Meanjin*,
64:4, 2008.

Christiansen, Peter & Ellender, Isabel, *People of the Merri Merri:
The Wurundjeri in Colonial Days*, Merri Creek Management

Committee, Melbourne, 2001.

Chicago Tribune and Los Angeles Times Travel Editors, 'Q&A with Lonely Planet Founders Tony & Maureen Wheeler', *Los Angeles Times*, 28 August 2007.

Clarke, Lorin, 'Like this little spirit that wafts': Contemporary Theatre in Australia, *Meanjin*, 69:1, 2010; 'Weeds are as important as trees': Where now for the Melbourne International Comedy Festival?' *Meanjin*, 70:1, 2011. Permission to quote courtesy of the author.

Coetzee, J.M., *Diary of a Bad Year*, Text Publishing, Melbourne, 2008. Permission to quote courtesy of the publisher, The Text Publishing Co Australia.

Croggon, Alison, 'The Williamson Syndrome', 1 July 2004; 'Review: Don Parties On', 16 January 2011, <www.theatrenotes.blogspot.com>. Permission to quote courtesy of the author.

CSIRO OzClim, <www.csiro.au/ozclim/home.do>,

Cutten History Committee, Fitzroy History Society (eds.), *Fitzroy, Melbourne's First Suburb*, Melbourne University Press, 1991. Permission to quote courtesy of the Fitzroy History Society.

Davidson, Jim, 'A Fugitive Art: An Interview with Barry Humphries', *Meanjin* 46:2, 1986; 'A Cork Upon the Ocean', *Meanjin*, 70:1, 2011. Permission to quote courtesy of the author.

Davis, Mark, 'Myths of the Generations: Baby Boomers, X and Y', *Overland*, no.198, 2007. Permission to quote courtesy of *Overland* and the author.

Davison, Graeme, *The Rise and Fall of Marvellous Melbourne*, Melbourne University Press, Melbourne, 1978. Permission to quote courtesy of the author.

Dawe, Bruce, 'Lifecycle', *Sometimes Gladness: Collected Poems 1954–2005*, Pearson Australia, Melbourne, 2006. Permission to quote courtesy of the author.

De Kretser, Michelle, 'Odds and endings', *Age*, 29 August 2009.

Permission to quote courtesy of the author.

Dobbin, Claire & Glow, Hilary, 'Women's Theatre and the APG: Interview', *Meanjin*, 55:2, 1984. Permission to quote courtesy of Hilary Glow.

Dubecki, Larissa, 'Rated R', *Age*, 23 November 2006. Permission to quote courtesy of the author.

Eltham, Ben, 'The Nicholas Building: A User's Manual', *Meanjin*, 69:3, 2010. Permission to quote courtesy of the author.

Enker, Debi, 'Hey Hey It's Divisive', *Sydney Morning Herald*, 10 April 2010.

Ferreter, Sarah, Lewis, Mike & Pickford, Mike, 'Melbourne's Revitalized Laneways', Melbourne, 2008.

Fitzgerald, Peter, 'The Historian in the Spotlight: Manning Clark's "History of Australia" – the Musical', in Stuart Macintyre & Sheila Fitzpatrick (eds.), *Against the Grain: Brian Fitzpatrick and Manning Clark in Australian History and Politics*, Melbourne University Press, Melbourne, 2007. Permission to quote courtesy of the author.

Flanagan, Martin, *1970 and Other Stories of the Australian Game*, McPhee Gribble, Melbourne, 1994.

Fraser, Carolyn, 'Notes on Provenance; or, Tom Ross's Tooth', *Meanjin*, 68:3, 2009. Permission to quote courtesy of the author.

Garner, Helen, *Monkey Grip*, McPhee Gribble, 1977; *The Children's Bach*, McPhee Gribble, Melbourne, 1984. Permission to quote courtesy of Penguin Books and the author. Penguin Books now publishes *Monkey Grip* (Melbourne, 2008) and *The Children's Bach* (Melbourne, 2008).

Gatto, Mick & Noble, Tom, *I, Gatto*, Melbourne University Publishing, Melbourne, 2009. Permission to quote courtesy of the publisher.

Gill, Raymond, 'City does give a rat's for Banksy's wiped-out art', *Age*, 28 April 2010.

Glickfeld, Elizabeth, 'Logophobia', *Meanjin*, 69:3, 2010. Permission to quote courtesy of the author.

Grant, Jane, 'Vultures on Every Bough', *Meanjin*, 63:1, 2004.

Grimwade, Stephen (ed), *Literary Melbourne: A Celebration of Writing and Ideas*, Hardie Grant, 2009.

Hamer, Michelle, 'A Hot Piece of History', *Age*, 5 February 2004.

Harden, Michael, *Melbourne: The Making of a Drinking and Eating Capital*, Hardie Grant Books, Melbourne, 2009; 'Unique and Deplorable: Regulating Drinking in Victoria', *Meanjin*, 69:3, 2010. Permission to quote courtesy of the publisher and the author.

Hardy, Marieke, 'The Slow Death of a Sticky Carpet', *The Drum*, 18 January 2010. Permission to quote courtesy of *The Drum* and the author.

Harmer, Wendy, 'Standing Up For Myself,' *Meanjin*, 55:2, 1984. Permission to quote courtesy of the author.

Hendrie, Doug, *Farrago*, 79:3, University of Melbourne, 2000.

Heyward, Michael, *The Ern Malley Affair*, UQP, St Lucia, 1993. Permission to quote courtesy of the author.

Hughes, Simon, 'At *Meanjin*, suddenly, nothing happened', *Crikey*, 13 June 2007.

Hutchinson, Garrie, 'The Funny Melbourne Television Phenomenon', *Meanjin*, 46:2, 1986. Permission to quote courtesy of the author.

Jillett, Neil, 'We were all wrong, Ava', *Age*, 14 January 1982.

Kelly, Declan, 'No Deaf Ears', *Meanjin*, 68:1, 2009. Permission to quote courtesy of the author.

Kelly, Paul, 'Leaps and Bounds', 1986; *How to Make Gravy*, Penguin Books, Melbourne, 2010. Permission to quote courtesy of Sony Music Publishing, Penguin Books and the author.

Kelly, Peter, *Buddha in a Bookshop*, Ulysses Press, Melbourne, 2007.

Ker, Paul, 'Yarra may face more depletion', *Age*, 23 May 2009.

Klugman, Matthew, 'Footy: The Season of Love, Faith and Agony', *Meanjin*, 68:3, 2009. Permission to quote courtesy of the author.

Lang, Lisa, *E.W. Cole: Chasing the Rainbow*, Arcade Publications, Melbourne, 2007. Permission to quote courtesy of the publisher.

Lee, Jenny, *Making Modern Melbourne*, Arcade Publications, Melbourne, 2008. Permission to quote courtesy of the publisher.

Lovett, Paris, 'The Italian Shop Closes', *Melbourne Times*, 1997. Permission to quote courtesy of the author.

McLaren, John, 'Time to Dream', *Meanjin*, 63:1, 2004.

McPhee, Hilary, *Other People's Words*, Picador, Sydney, 2001; 'Survival Struggles', *Meanjin* 63:1, 2004; 'Timid Minds', *Meanjin*, 69:4, 2010. Permission to quote courtesy of the author.

Macainsh, Greg, 'The Fender L', *Meanjin*, 65:3, 2006. Permission to quote courtesy of the author.

Maloney, Shane, *The Brush-Off*, Text Publishing, 1996. Permission to quote courtesy of the author and the publisher, The Text Publishing Co Australia.

Mares, Peter, 'Nam Le – *The Boat*', *The Book Show*, ABC Radio National, 18 June 2008. Permission to quote courtesy of *The Book Show* and Nam Le.

Martin, Tony, 'Party like it's 1991', *The Scrivener's Fancy*, 31 March 2010. Permission to quote courtesy of the author.

Matthews, Brian, *A Fine and Private Place*, Pan Macmillan, Sydney, 2000; *Manning Clark: A Life*, Allen & Unwin, Sydney, 2008.

Mees, Paul, 'Kosky was a transport apologist, not a reformer', *Sydney Morning Herald*, 18 January 2010.

Mews, Peter, *Bright Planet*, Picador, Sydney, 2004. Permission to quote courtesy of the author.

Miletic, Daniella, 'Bittersweet taste as institution shuts shop', *Age*, 21 May 2010.

Money, Lawrence, 'McQueen of Melbourne's movers and shakers', *Age*, 18 November 2009.

Moses, Alexa, 'Unleash the inner animal', *Sydney Morning Herald*, 18 December 2004.

Murnane, Gerald, *Tamarisk Row*, Giramondo Publishing, 2008. Permission to quote courtesy of the publisher.

Nguyen, Thuy Linh, 'Footscray Whitewash', *Peril: Asian-Australian Arts and Culture Magazine*, no. 10, 5 January 2011, <www.peril.com.au>. Permission to quote courtesy of *Peril* and the author.

Nichols, David, 'The Uncultured Herd and Us', *Meanjin*, 67:3, 2008; 'Rebuild, better than ever', *Age*, 16 February 2009; 'In the Outer: Doveton', *Meanjin*, 69:3, 2010. Permission to quote courtesy of the author.

Northover, Kylie, 'Banksy's first Australian interview', *Age*, 29 May 2010.

O'Brien, Simon & Malatt, Peter 'Episode 2: The Public Good', *In the Mind of the Architect*, ABC TV and The Space, 2000.

O'Hanlon, Seamus, *Melbourne Remade: The Inner City Since the Seventies*, Arcade Publications, 2010. Permission to quote courtesy of the publisher.

Otto, Kristin, *Yarra: A Diverting History of Melbourne's Murky River*, Text Publishing, Melbourne, 2005. Permission to quote courtesy of the author and the publisher, The Text Publishing Co Australia.

Peel, Victoria, Yule, Jane & Zion, Deborah, *A History of Hawthorn*, Melbourne University Press, Melbourne, 1993. Permission to quote courtesy of the authors.

Perkins, Rachel & Langton, Marcia (eds.), *First Australians*, Melbourne University Publishing, Melbourne, 2008.

Presland, Gary, *The First Peoples of Melbourne, Port Phillip and Central Victoria: The Eastern Kulin*, Museum Victoria Publishing, Melbourne, 2010.

Roach, Archie, 'Charcoal Lane'. Permission to quote courtesy of Mushroom Music Publishing and the author.

Roberts, Bev, 'Re-opening a volcano', *Floreo*, no. 21, Autumn 2010, Royal Botanic Gardens, Melbourne. Permission to quote courtesy of the publisher and the author.

Selinger-Morris, Samantha,' Clowning around with big issues', *Sydney Morning Herald*, 29 December 2009.

Silvester, John, 'Who stole Eloise?', *Age*, 5 July 2003.

Sparrow, Jeff & Sparrow, Jill, *Radical Melbourne*, Vulgar Press, Melbourne, 2001 and *Radical Melbourne 2*, Vulgar Press, Melbourne, 2004. Permission to quote courtesy of the authors.

Steger, Jason, 'A very Melbourne man collects literary prize', *Age*, 12 November 2009.

Styant-Browne, Anthony, 'Arrivista', *Architecture Australia*, May/June 1999.

Temple, Peter, *Truth*, Text Publishing, 2009. Permission to quote courtesy of the author and the publisher, The Text Publishing Co Australia.

Tsiolkas, Christos, *The Slap*, Allen & Unwin, Crows Nest, 2008. Permission to quote courtesy of the publisher and the author.

Turner, George, *The Sea and Summer*, Faber and Faber, London, 1987.

Walker, Clinton J. & McIntyre, Tanya, 'Artless Mad Fun,' *Meanjin*, 69:3, 2010. Permission to quote courtesy of Clinton J. Walker.

Weaver, Rachael, 'Waxwork', *Meanjin*, 68:3, 2009. Permission to quote courtesy of the author.

Wells, Dianna, 'On Edge', *Meanjin*, 69:3, 2010. Permission to quote courtesy of the author.

West, Rosemary, 'We need more green areas, not people', *Age*, 11 January 2010.

Williams, Luke, 'Public transport: rebadging OK, but rebadgering of passengers is not', *Crikey*, 4 December 2009.

Wilmoth, Peter, *Glad All Over: The Countdown Years 1974–1987*, McPhee Gribble, Melbourne, 1993; 'Life after Mietta', *Age*, 25 July 2004 ; 'The '70s stripped bare', *Age*, 17 July 2005. Permission to quote courtesy of the author.

Zable, Arnold, *Café Scheherazade*, Text Publishing, Melbourne, 2003. Permission to quote courtesy of the publisher, The Text Publishing Co Australia.

Acknowledgements

I quote a lot of people in this book because I want it to reflect the city as I experience it, as a city of conversations. You'll notice that the same names come up time and time again: commentators, artists, writers, family and friends such as Saul Cunningham, Carolyn Fraser, Paul Kelly, Hilary McPhee, Virginia Murdoch, David Nichols and Jeff Sparrow. These people are my peers, and their work and our conversations are a part of the fabric of my city. They were also key readers, and their editorial feedback as I was writing was invaluable.

My broader community of writing friends has also been crucial. They are represented, in part, by the many *Meanjin* articles I have quoted from, articles published during the time I was editor of the journal. On this front I am particularly in debt to Ciannon Cazaly, Lorin Clarke, Jim Davidson, Ben Eltham, Elizabeth Glickfeld, Declan Kelly, Matthew Klugman, Dianna Wells and Marcus Westbury.

Graeme Blundell was especially generous with his time, as were Bruce and Ann McGregor. Tim Richards and Helen Garner were generous with their emails. I would also like to thank Jessica Au, Stuart Geddes, Emily Kiddell and Richard McGregor for their support while I was writing this book. I'd particularly like to thank the gloriously named Natalie Book, who went above and beyond the call of duty while copyediting *Melbourne*.

Finally, thanks to Phillipa McGuinness, my publisher at UNSW Press, whose idea this book was in the first place.